D0577317

Out of the BLUE™

VOLUME ONE

GARTH ENNIS
KEITH BURNS

JASON WORDIE
ROB STEEN

AFTERSHOCK™

GARTH ENNIS writer & co-creator

KEITH BURNS artist & co-creator

JASON WORDIE colorist

ROB STEEN letterer

KEITH BURNS cover

CHARLES PRITCHETT book designer and production

JARED K. FLETCHER logo designer

JOE PRUETT editor

AFTERSHOCK™

MIKE MARTS - Editor-in-Chief ● **JOE PRUETT** - Publisher/Chief Creative Officer ● **LEE KRAMER** - President
JON KRAMER - Chief Executive Officer ● **STEVE ROTTERDAM** - SVP, Sales & Marketing ● **BLAKE STOCKER** - Chief Financial Officer
CHRISTINA HARRINGTON - Managing Editor ● **LISA Y. WU** - Retailer/Fan Relations Manager
STEPHANIE CASEBIER & SARAH PRUETT - Publishing Assistants ● **TEDDY LEO** - Editorial Assistant
CHARLES PRITCHETT - Comics Production ● **COREY BREEN** - Collections Production

AfterShock Logo Design by **COMICRAFT**
Publicity: contact **AARON MARION** (aaron@publichausagency.com) & **RYAN CROY** (ryan@publichausagency.com)
Special thanks to **MARINE KSADZHIKYAN, IRA KURGAN, ANTONIA LIANOS, STEPHAN NILSON & JULIE PIFHER**

OUT OF THE BLUE: VOLUME ONE Published by AfterShock Comics, LLC, 15300 Ventura Boulevard Suite 507, Sherman Oaks, CA 91403. Copyright © 2019 by Spitfire Productions and AfterShock Comics. Out of the Blue™ (including all prominent characters featured herein), its logo and all character likeness are trademarks of Spitfire Productions and AfterShock Comics, unless otherwise noted. All rights reserved. AfterShock Comics and its logos are trademarks of AfterShock Comics, LLC. No part of this publication may be reproduced or transmitted, in any form or by any means (except for short excerpts for review purposes) without the expressed written permission of AfterShock Comics, LLC. All names, characters, events and locales in this publication are entirely fictional. Any resemblance to actual persons (living or dead), events or places, without satiric intent, is coincidental. PRINTED IN KOREA.
First Printing: March 2019. 10 9 8 7 6 5 4 3 2 1

AFTERSHOCKCOMICS.COM Follow us on social media

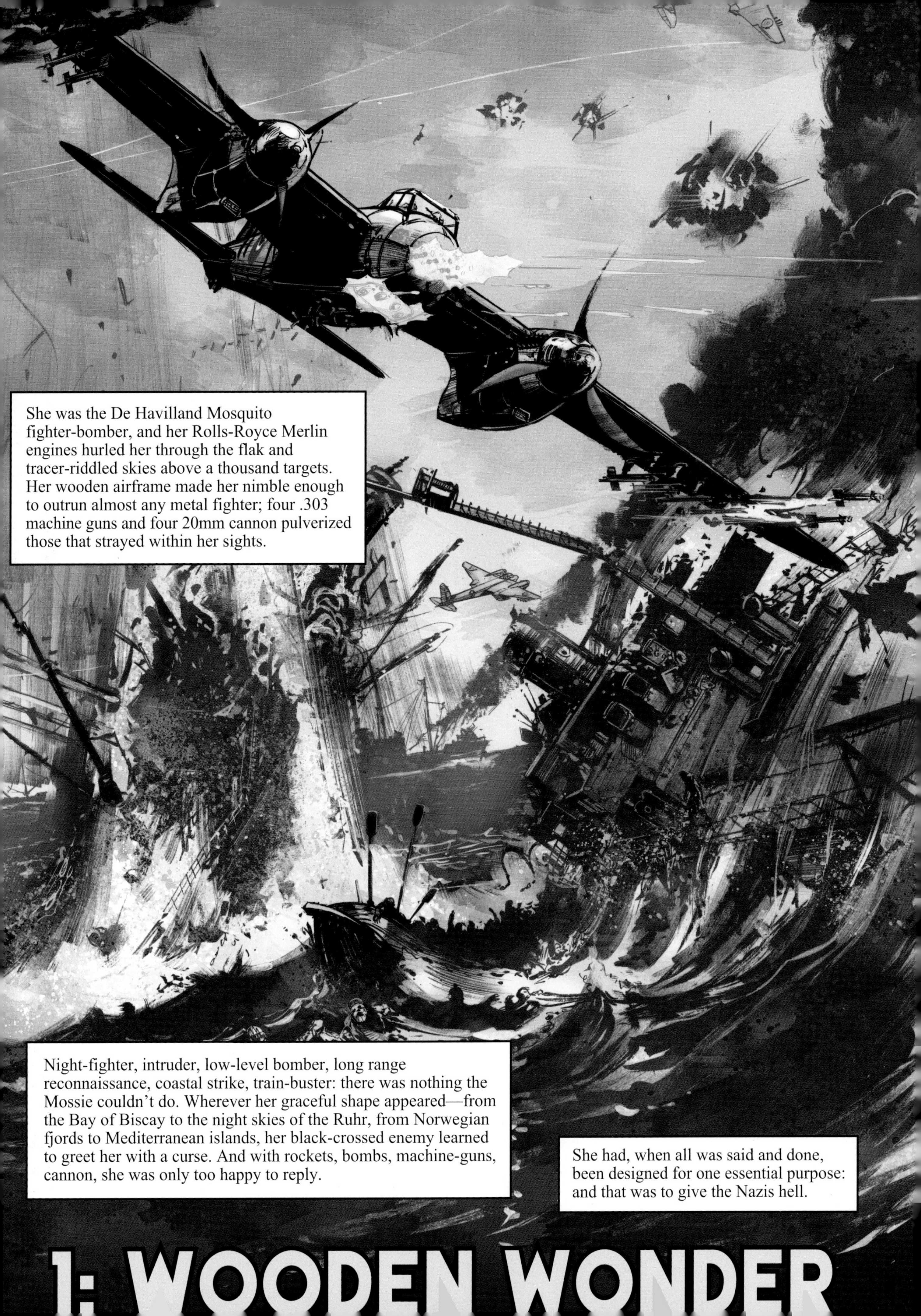
She was the De Havilland Mosquito fighter-bomber, and her Rolls-Royce Merlin engines hurled her through the flak and tracer-riddled skies above a thousand targets. Her wooden airframe made her nimble enough to outrun almost any metal fighter; four .303 machine guns and four 20mm cannon pulverized those that strayed within her sights.
Night-fighter, intruder, low-level bomber, long range reconnaissance, coastal strike, train-buster: there was nothing the Mossie couldn't do. Wherever her graceful shape appeared—from the Bay of Biscay to the night skies of the Ruhr, from Norwegian fjords to Mediterranean islands, her black-crossed enemy learned to greet her with a curse. And with rockets, bombs, machine-guns, cannon, she was only too happy to reply.
She had, when all was said and done, been designed for one essential purpose: and that was to give the Nazis hell.
1: WOODEN WONDER

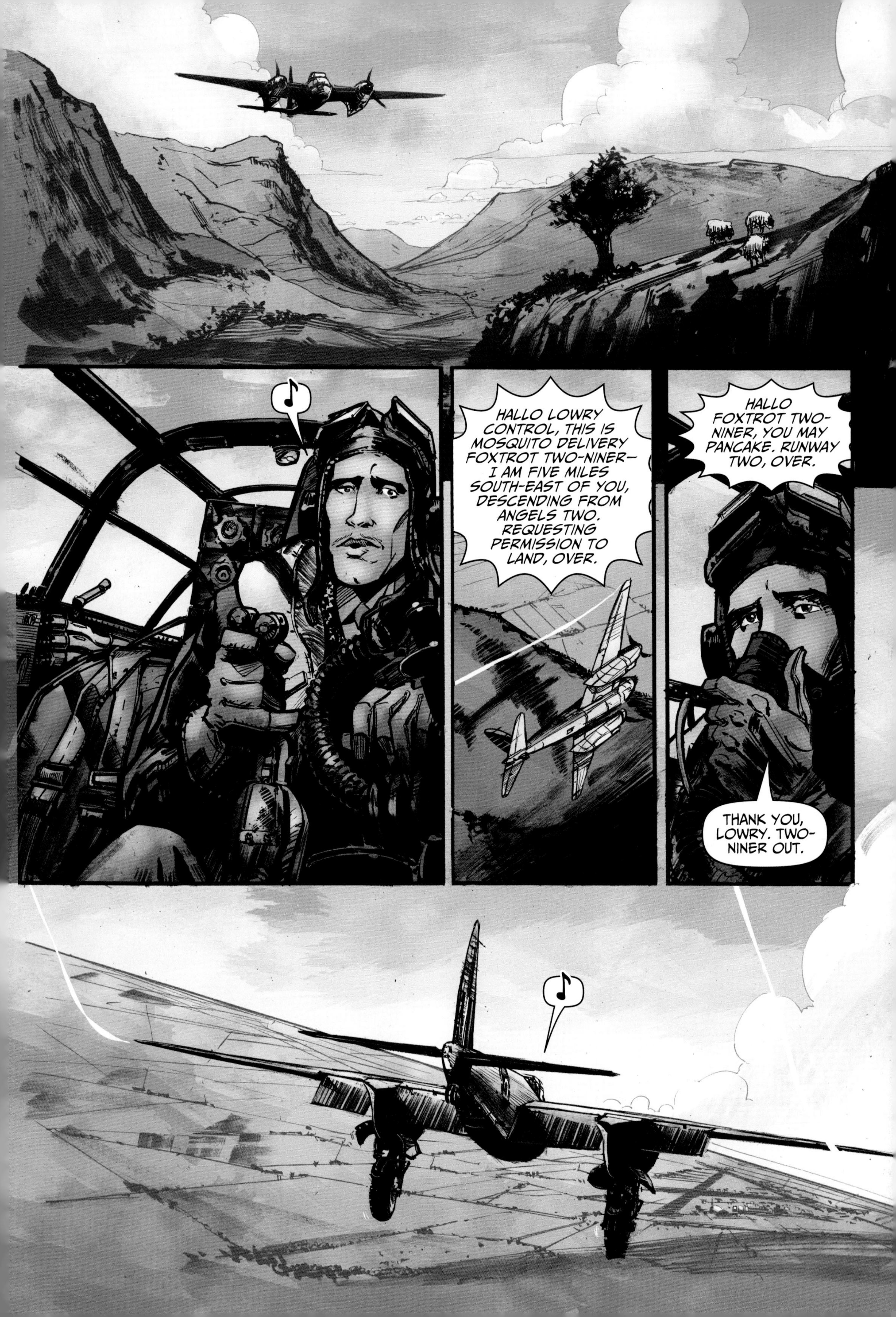
♪
HALLO LOWRY CONTROL, THIS IS MOSQUITO DELIVERY FOXTROT TWO-NINER– I AM FIVE MILES SOUTH-EAST OF YOU, DESCENDING FROM ANGELS TWO. REQUESTING PERMISSION TO LAND, OVER.
HALLO FOXTROT TWO-NINER, YOU MAY PANCAKE. RUNWAY TWO, OVER.
THANK YOU, LOWRY. TWO-NINER OUT.
♪

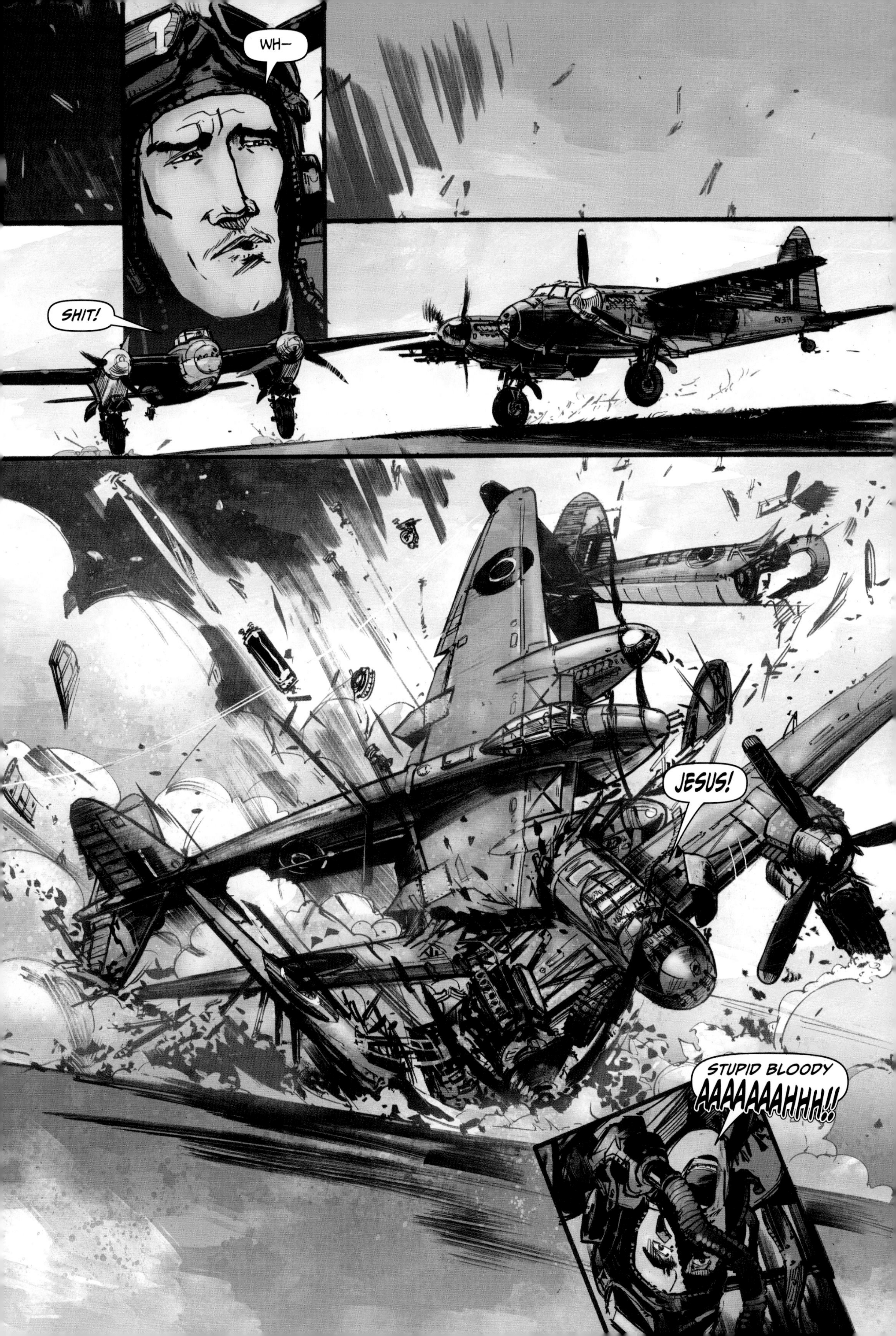
WH–
SHIT!
JESUS!
STUPID BLOODY AAAAAAAHHH!!

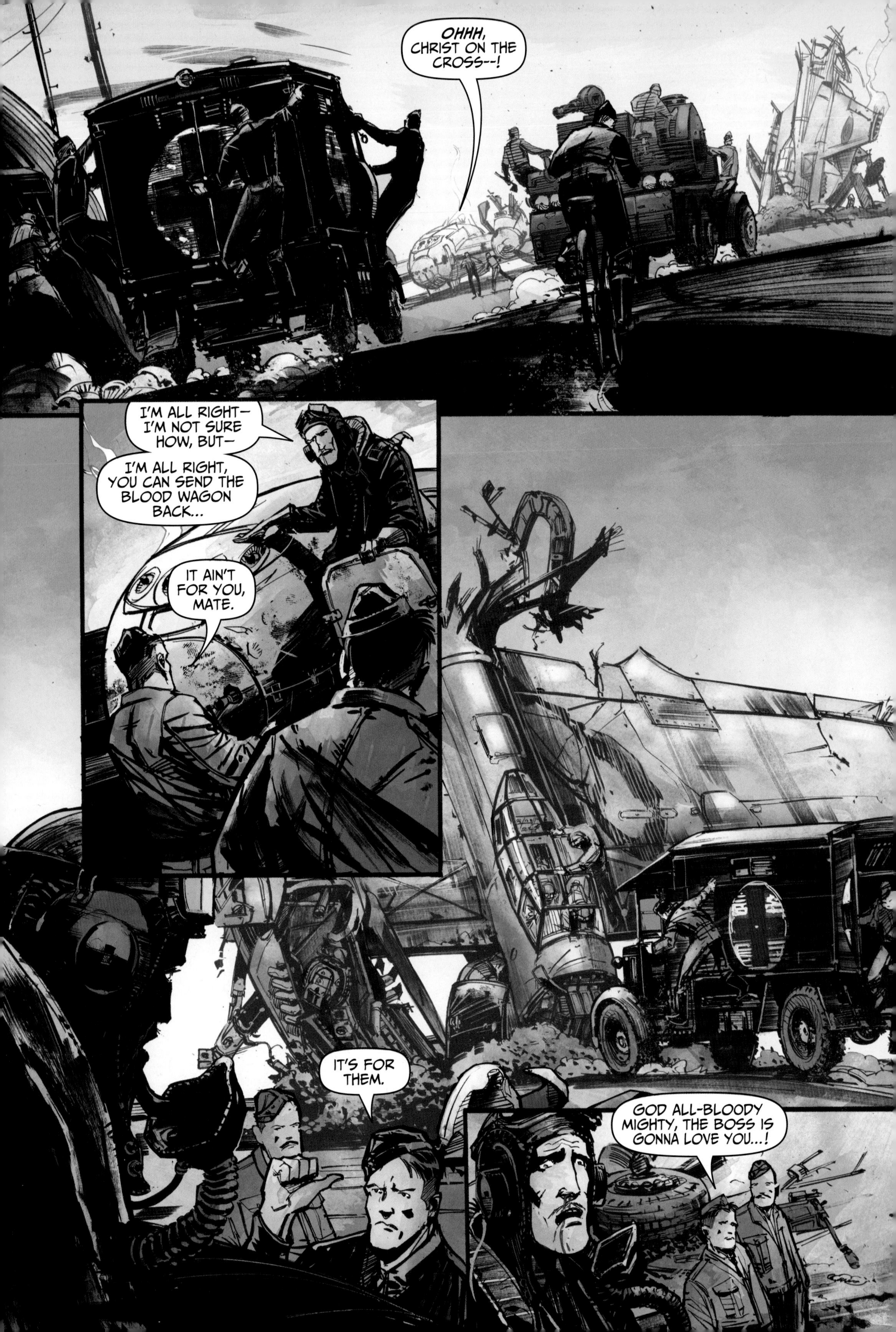
OHHH, CHRIST ON THE CROSS--!
I'M ALL RIGHT— I'M NOT SURE HOW, BUT—
I'M ALL RIGHT, YOU CAN SEND THE BLOOD WAGON BACK...
IT AIN'T FOR YOU, MATE.
IT'S FOR THEM.
GOD ALL-BLOODY MIGHTY, THE BOSS IS GONNA LOVE YOU...!

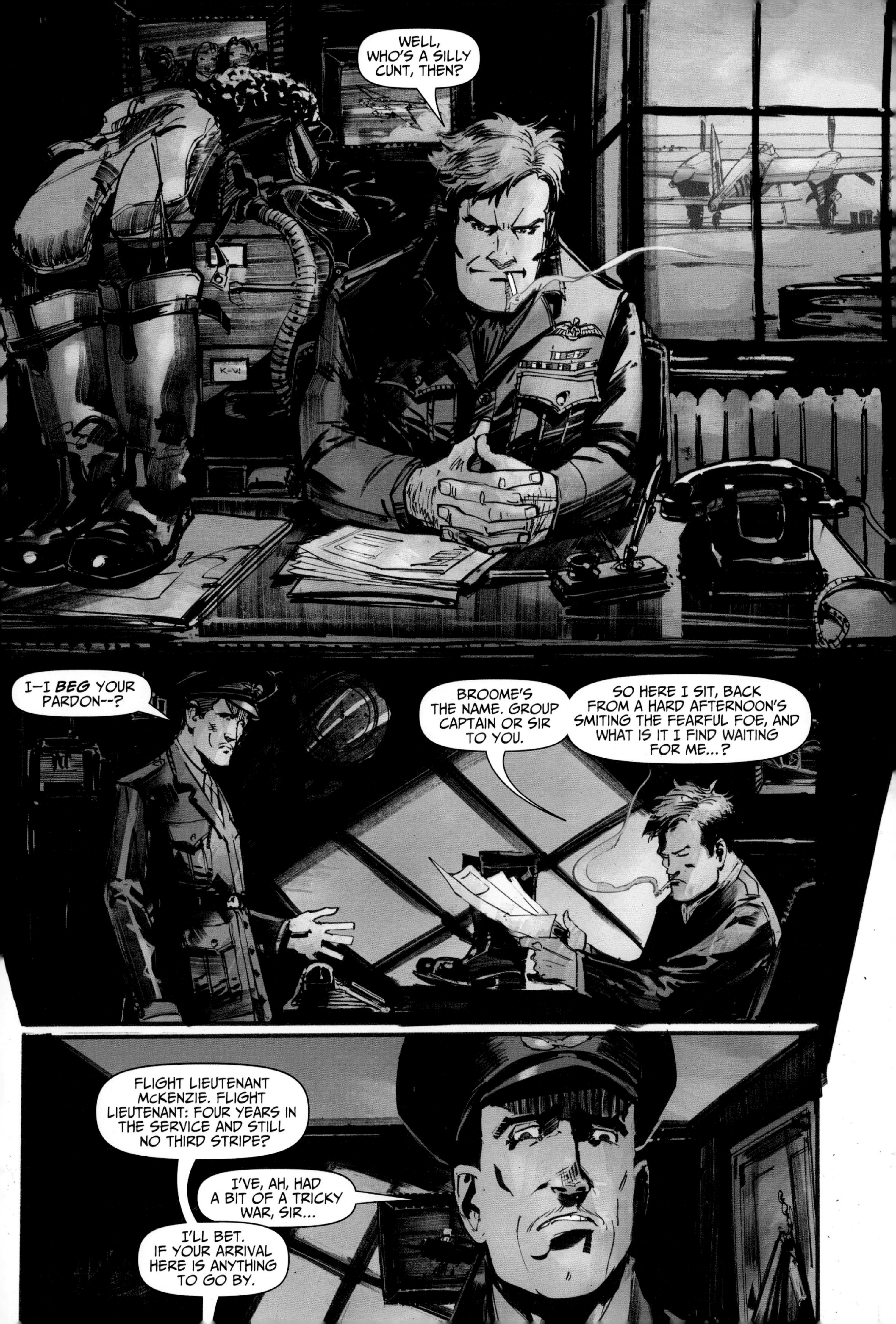
WELL, WHO'S A SILLY CUNT, THEN?
K-W
I--I **BEG** YOUR PARDON--?
BROOME'S THE NAME. GROUP CAPTAIN OR SIR TO YOU.
SO HERE I SIT, BACK FROM A HARD AFTERNOON'S SMITING THE FEARFUL FOE, AND WHAT IS IT I FIND WAITING FOR ME...?
FLIGHT LIEUTENANT McKENZIE. FLIGHT LIEUTENANT: FOUR YEARS IN THE SERVICE AND STILL NO THIRD STRIPE?
I'VE, AH, HAD A BIT OF A TRICKY WAR, SIR...
I'LL BET. IF YOUR ARRIVAL HERE IS ANYTHING TO GO BY.

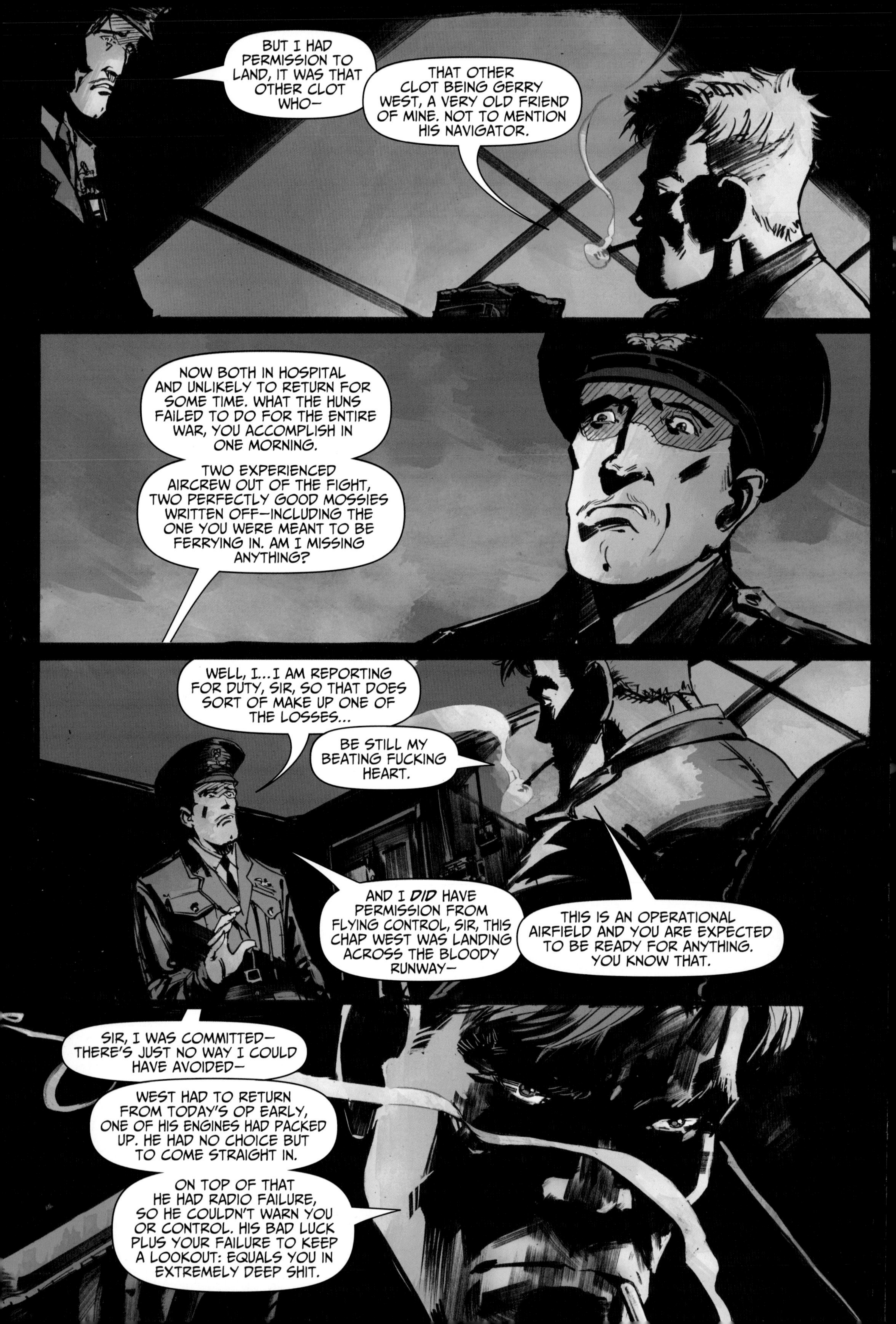
BUT I HAD PERMISSION TO LAND, IT WAS THAT OTHER CLOT WHO–
THAT OTHER CLOT BEING GERRY WEST, A VERY OLD FRIEND OF MINE. NOT TO MENTION HIS NAVIGATOR.
NOW BOTH IN HOSPITAL AND UNLIKELY TO RETURN FOR SOME TIME. WHAT THE HUNS FAILED TO DO FOR THE ENTIRE WAR, YOU ACCOMPLISH IN ONE MORNING.
TWO EXPERIENCED AIRCREW OUT OF THE FIGHT, TWO PERFECTLY GOOD MOSSIES WRITTEN OFF–INCLUDING THE ONE YOU WERE MEANT TO BE FERRYING IN. AM I MISSING ANYTHING?
WELL, I...I AM REPORTING FOR DUTY, SIR, SO THAT DOES SORT OF MAKE UP ONE OF THE LOSSES...
BE STILL MY BEATING FUCKING HEART.
AND I *DID* HAVE PERMISSION FROM FLYING CONTROL, SIR, THIS CHAP WEST WAS LANDING ACROSS THE BLOODY RUNWAY–
THIS IS AN OPERATIONAL AIRFIELD AND YOU ARE EXPECTED TO BE READY FOR ANYTHING. YOU KNOW THAT.
SIR, I WAS COMMITTED– THERE'S JUST NO WAY I COULD HAVE AVOIDED–
WEST HAD TO RETURN FROM TODAY'S OP EARLY, ONE OF HIS ENGINES HAD PACKED UP. HE HAD NO CHOICE BUT TO COME STRAIGHT IN.
ON TOP OF THAT HE HAD RADIO FAILURE, SO HE COULDN'T WARN YOU OR CONTROL. HIS BAD LUCK PLUS YOUR FAILURE TO KEEP A LOOKOUT: EQUALS YOU IN EXTREMELY DEEP SHIT.

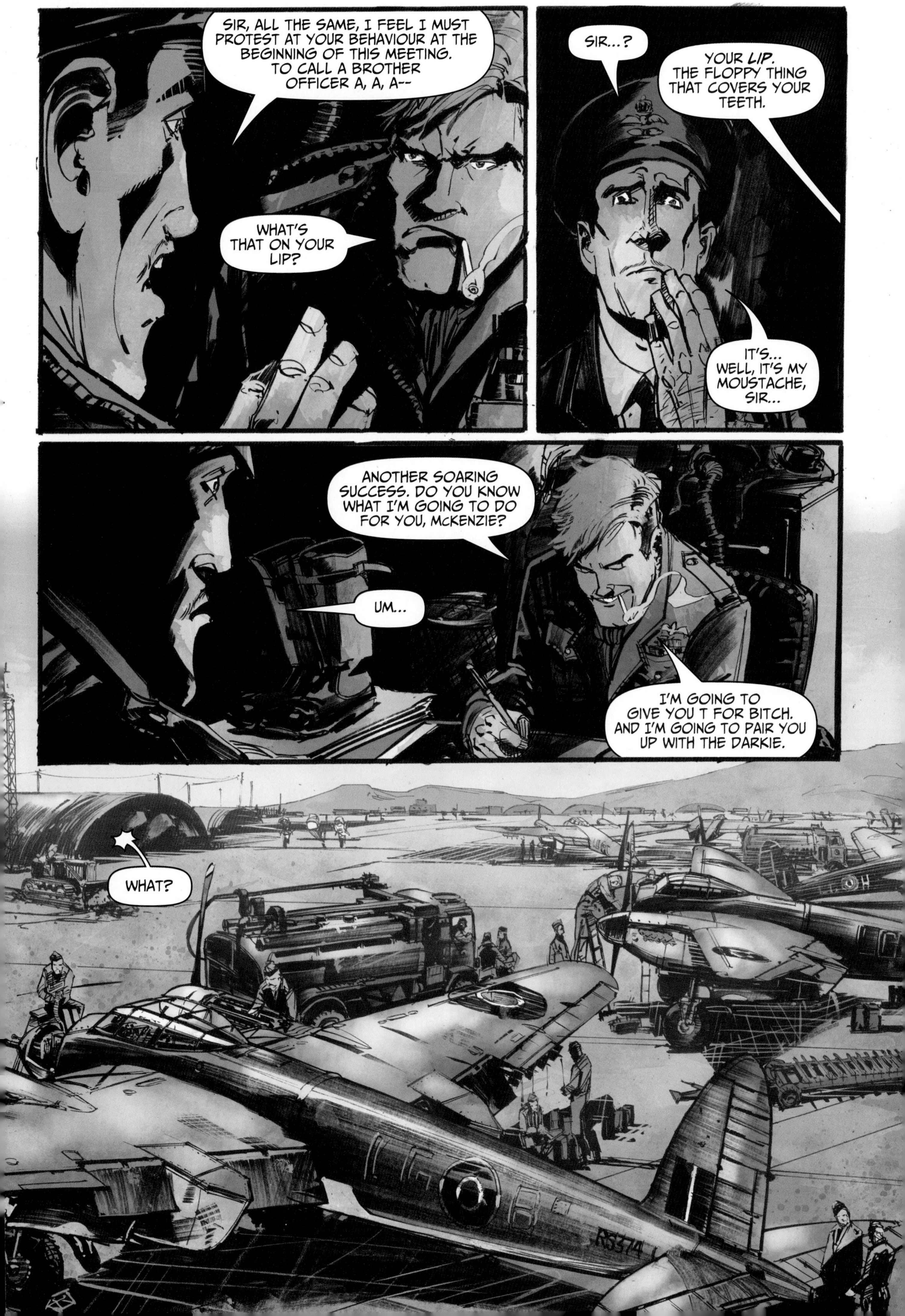
SIR, ALL THE SAME, I FEEL I MUST PROTEST AT YOUR BEHAVIOUR AT THE BEGINNING OF THIS MEETING. TO CALL A BROTHER OFFICER A, A, A--
WHAT'S THAT ON YOUR LIP?
SIR...?
YOUR *LIP*. THE FLOPPY THING THAT COVERS YOUR TEETH.
IT'S... WELL, IT'S MY MOUSTACHE, SIR...
ANOTHER SOARING SUCCESS. DO YOU KNOW WHAT I'M GOING TO DO FOR YOU, McKENZIE?
UM...
I'M GOING TO GIVE YOU T FOR BITCH. AND I'M GOING TO PAIR YOU UP WITH THE DARKIE.
WHAT?
R5374

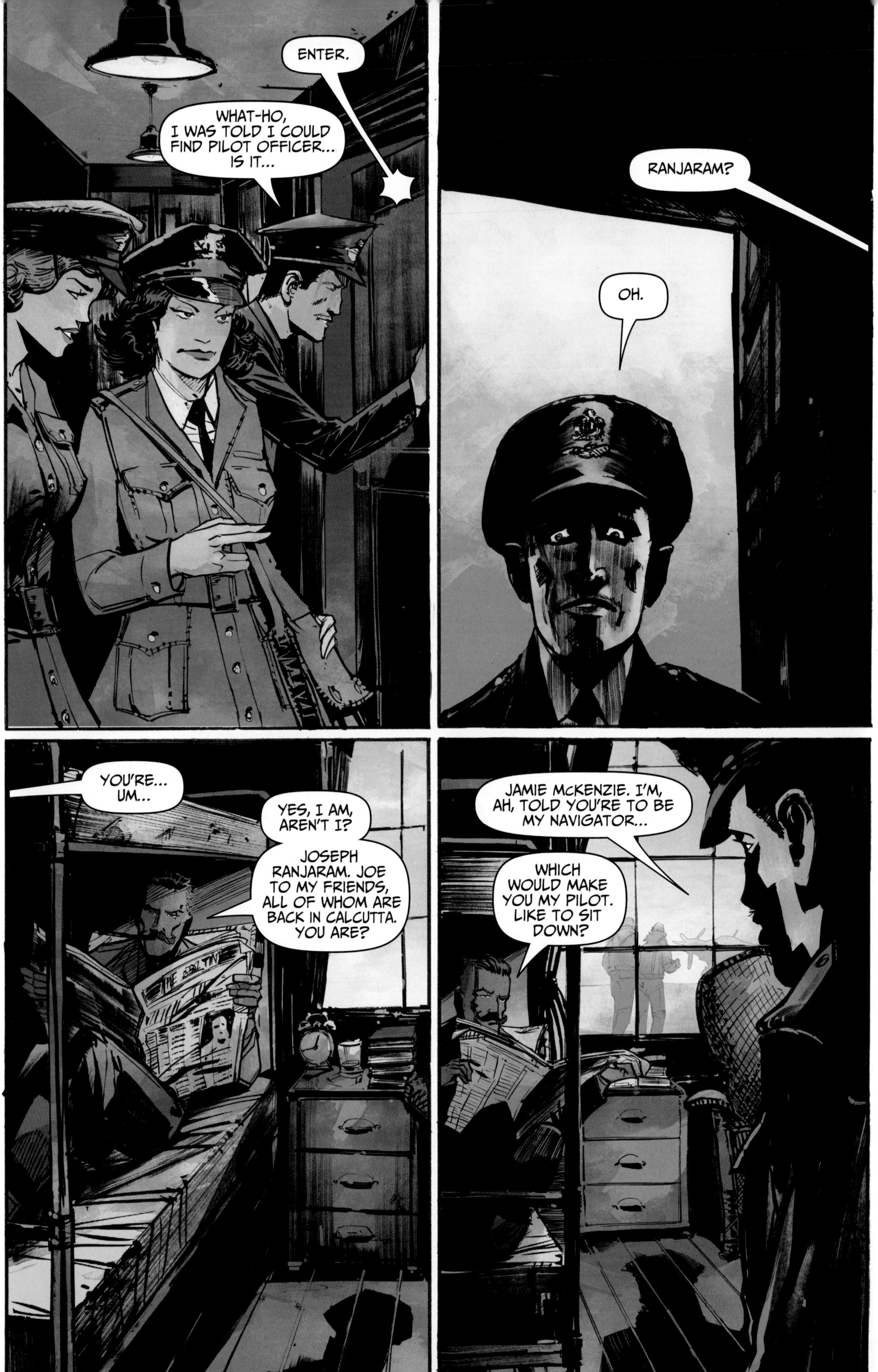
ENTER.
WHAT-HO, I WAS TOLD I COULD FIND PILOT OFFICER... IS IT...
RANJARAM?
OH.
YOU'RE... UM...
YES, I AM, AREN'T I?
JOSEPH RANJARAM. JOE TO MY FRIENDS, ALL OF WHOM ARE BACK IN CALCUTTA. YOU ARE?
JAMIE McKENZIE. I'M, AH, TOLD YOU'RE TO BE MY NAVIGATOR...
WHICH WOULD MAKE YOU MY PILOT. LIKE TO SIT DOWN?

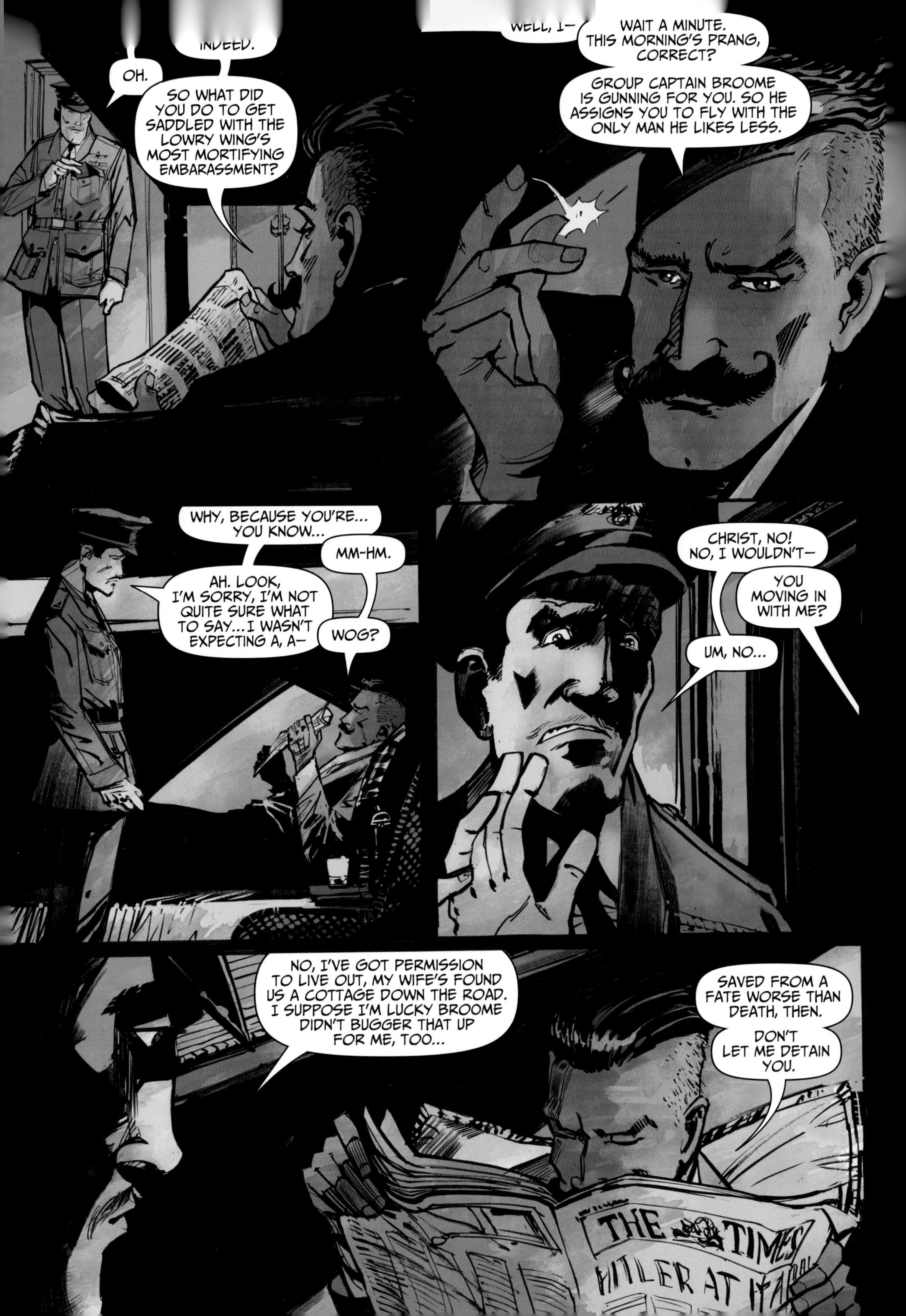
OH.
INDEED.
SO WHAT DID YOU DO TO GET SADDLED WITH THE LOWRY WING'S MOST MORTIFYING EMBARASSMENT?
WELL, I—
WAIT A MINUTE. THIS MORNING'S PRANG, CORRECT?
GROUP CAPTAIN BROOME IS GUNNING FOR YOU. SO HE ASSIGNS YOU TO FLY WITH THE ONLY MAN HE LIKES LESS.
WHY, BECAUSE YOU'RE... YOU KNOW...
MM-HM.
AH. LOOK, I'M SORRY, I'M NOT QUITE SURE WHAT TO SAY...I WASN'T EXPECTING A, A—
WOG?
CHRIST, NO! NO, I WOULDN'T—
YOU MOVING IN WITH ME?
UM, NO...
NO, I'VE GOT PERMISSION TO LIVE OUT, MY WIFE'S FOUND US A COTTAGE DOWN THE ROAD. I SUPPOSE I'M LUCKY BROOME DIDN'T BUGGER THAT UP FOR ME, TOO...
SAVED FROM A FATE WORSE THAN DEATH, THEN.
DON'T LET ME DETAIN YOU.
THE TIMES
HITLER AT

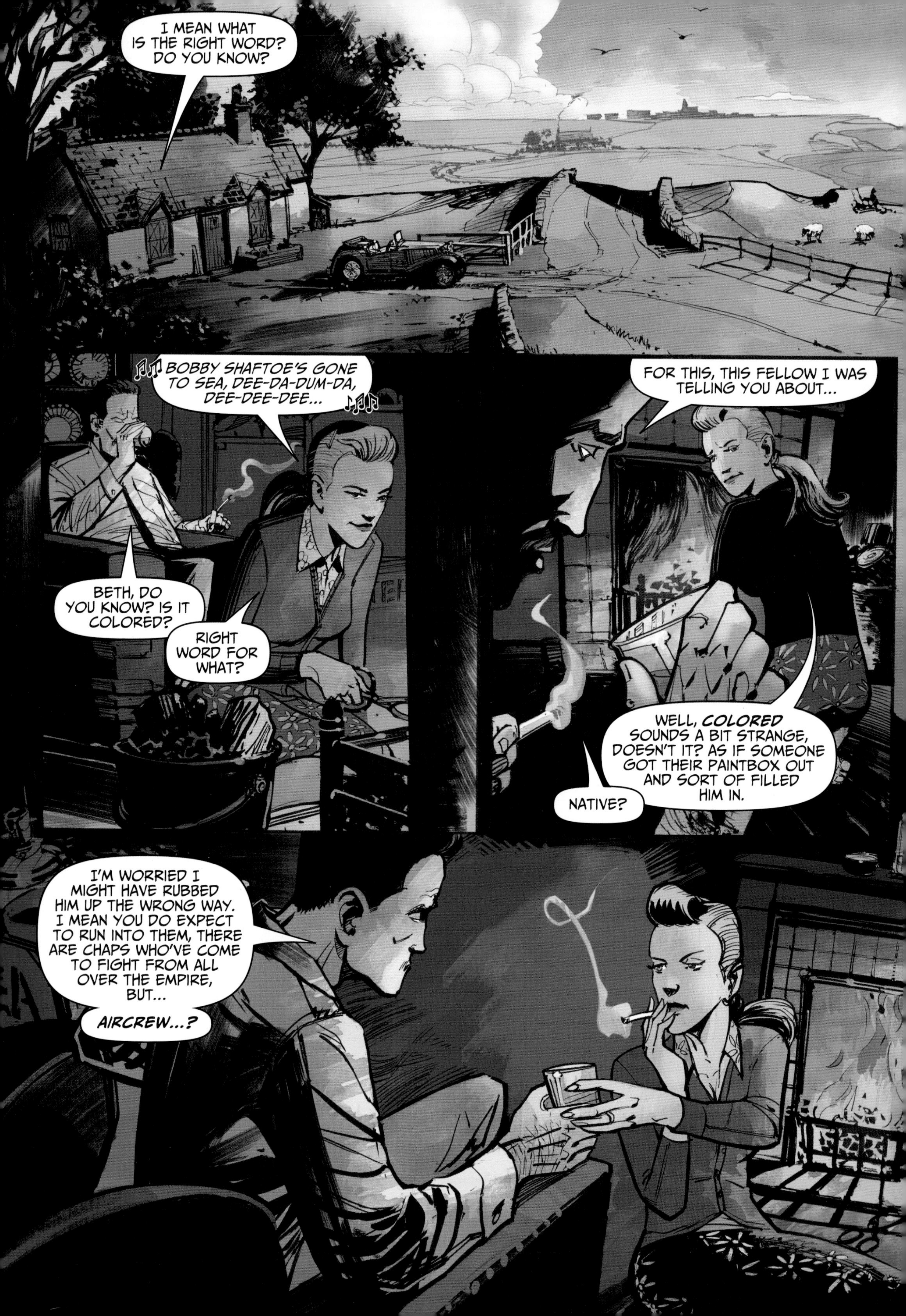
I MEAN WHAT IS THE RIGHT WORD? DO YOU KNOW?
BOBBY SHAFTOE'S GONE TO SEA, DEE-DA-DUM-DA, DEE-DEE-DEE...
BETH, DO YOU KNOW? IS IT COLORED?
RIGHT WORD FOR WHAT?
FOR THIS, THIS FELLOW I WAS TELLING YOU ABOUT...
WELL, COLORED SOUNDS A BIT STRANGE, DOESN'T IT? AS IF SOMEONE GOT THEIR PAINTBOX OUT AND SORT OF FILLED HIM IN.
NATIVE?
I'M WORRIED I MIGHT HAVE RUBBED HIM UP THE WRONG WAY. I MEAN YOU DO EXPECT TO RUN INTO THEM, THERE ARE CHAPS WHO'VE COME TO FIGHT FROM ALL OVER THE EMPIRE, BUT...
AIRCREW...?

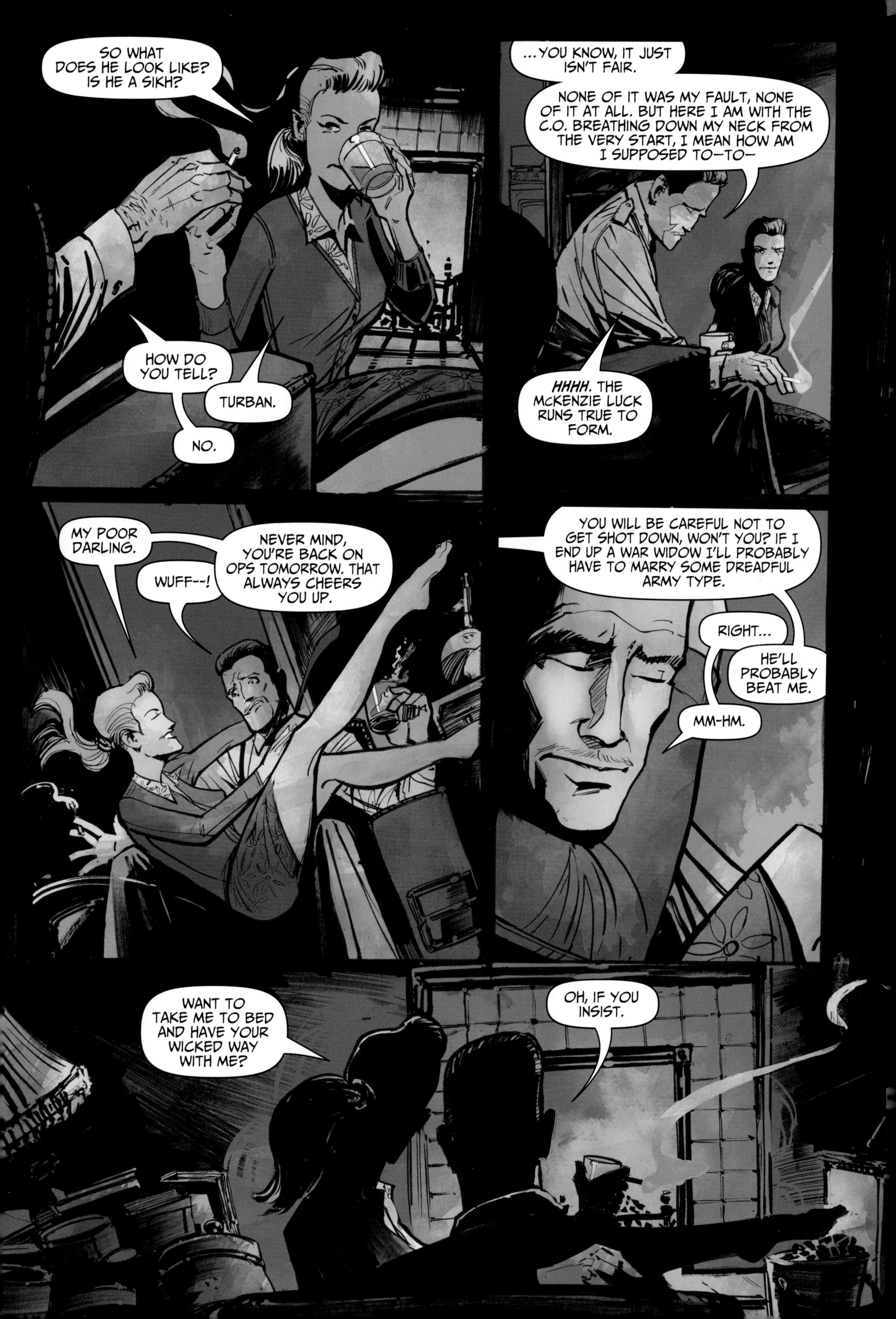
SO WHAT DOES HE LOOK LIKE? IS HE A SIKH?
HOW DO YOU TELL?
TURBAN.
NO.
...YOU KNOW, IT JUST ISN'T FAIR.
NONE OF IT WAS MY FAULT, NONE OF IT AT ALL. BUT HERE I AM WITH THE C.O. BREATHING DOWN MY NECK FROM THE VERY START, I MEAN HOW AM I SUPPOSED TO—TO—
HHHH. THE McKENZIE LUCK RUNS TRUE TO FORM.
MY POOR DARLING.
WUFF--!
NEVER MIND, YOU'RE BACK ON OPS TOMORROW. THAT ALWAYS CHEERS YOU UP.
YOU WILL BE CAREFUL NOT TO GET SHOT DOWN, WON'T YOU? IF I END UP A WAR WIDOW I'LL PROBABLY HAVE TO MARRY SOME DREADFUL ARMY TYPE.
RIGHT...
HE'LL PROBABLY BEAT ME.
MM-HM.
WANT TO TAKE ME TO BED AND HAVE YOUR WICKED WAY WITH ME?
OH, IF YOU INSIST.

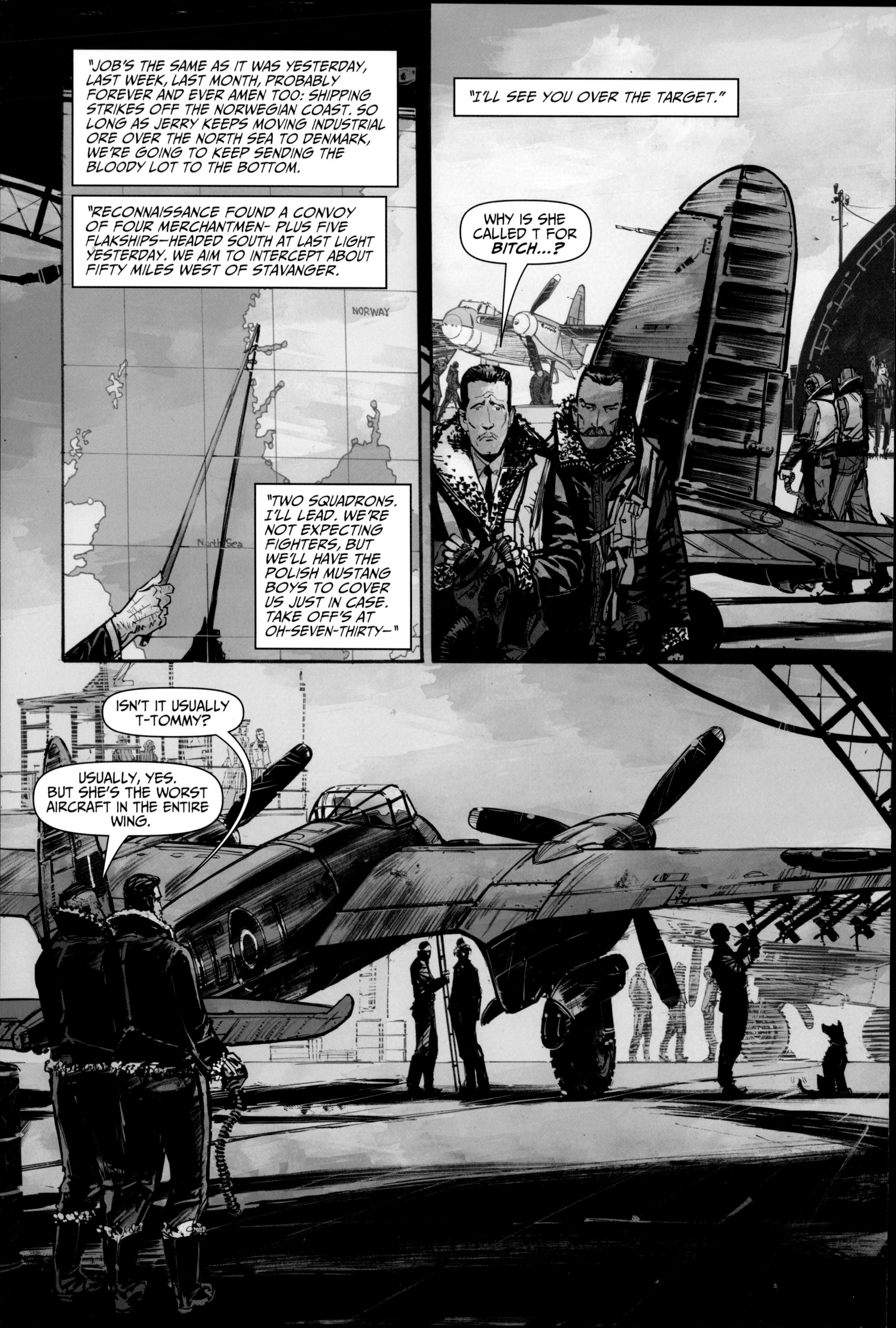
"JOB'S THE SAME AS IT WAS YESTERDAY, LAST WEEK, LAST MONTH, PROBABLY FOREVER AND EVER AMEN TOO: SHIPPING STRIKES OFF THE NORWEGIAN COAST. SO LONG AS JERRY KEEPS MOVING INDUSTRIAL ORE OVER THE NORTH SEA TO DENMARK, WE'RE GOING TO KEEP SENDING THE BLOODY LOT TO THE BOTTOM.
"RECONNAISSANCE FOUND A CONVOY OF FOUR MERCHANTMEN- PLUS FIVE FLAKSHIPS—HEADED SOUTH AT LAST LIGHT YESTERDAY. WE AIM TO INTERCEPT ABOUT FIFTY MILES WEST OF STAVANGER.
NORWAY
North Sea
"TWO SQUADRONS. I'LL LEAD. WE'RE NOT EXPECTING FIGHTERS, BUT WE'LL HAVE THE POLISH MUSTANG BOYS TO COVER US JUST IN CASE. TAKE OFF'S AT OH-SEVEN-THIRTY—"
"I'LL SEE YOU OVER THE TARGET."
WHY IS SHE CALLED T FOR BITCH...?
ISN'T IT USUALLY T-TOMMY?
USUALLY, YES. BUT SHE'S THE WORST AIRCRAFT IN THE ENTIRE WING.

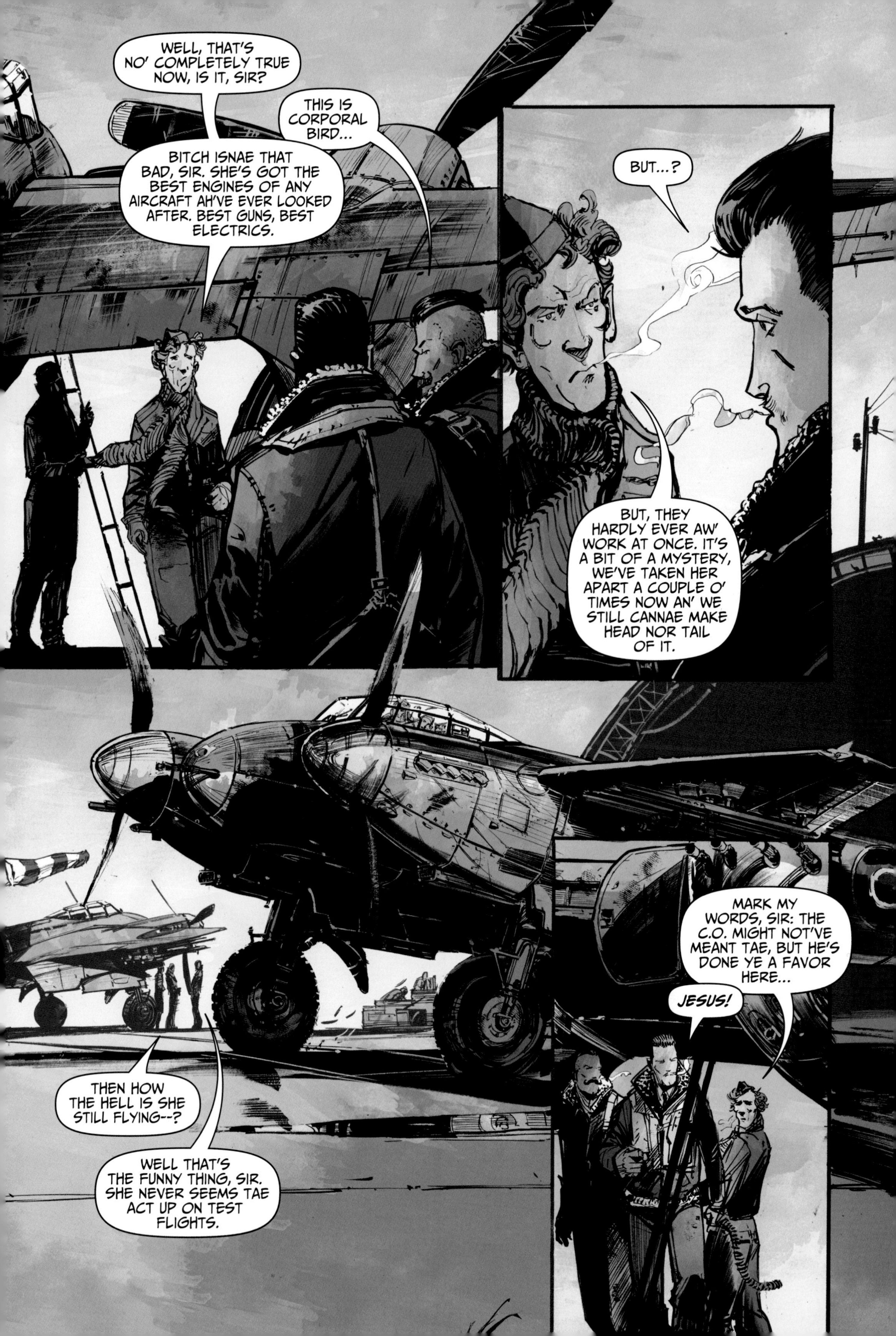
WELL, THAT'S NO' COMPLETELY TRUE NOW, IS IT, SIR?
THIS IS CORPORAL BIRD...
BITCH ISNAE THAT BAD, SIR. SHE'S GOT THE BEST ENGINES OF ANY AIRCRAFT AH'VE EVER LOOKED AFTER. BEST GUNS, BEST ELECTRICS.
BUT...?
BUT, THEY HARDLY EVER AW' WORK AT ONCE. IT'S A BIT OF A MYSTERY, WE'VE TAKEN HER APART A COUPLE O' TIMES NOW AN' WE STILL CANNAE MAKE HEAD NOR TAIL OF IT.
THEN HOW THE HELL IS SHE STILL FLYING--?
WELL THAT'S THE FUNNY THING, SIR. SHE NEVER SEEMS TAE ACT UP ON TEST FLIGHTS.
MARK MY WORDS, SIR: THE C.O. MIGHT NOT'VE MEANT TAE, BUT HE'S DONE YE A FAVOR HERE...
JESUS!

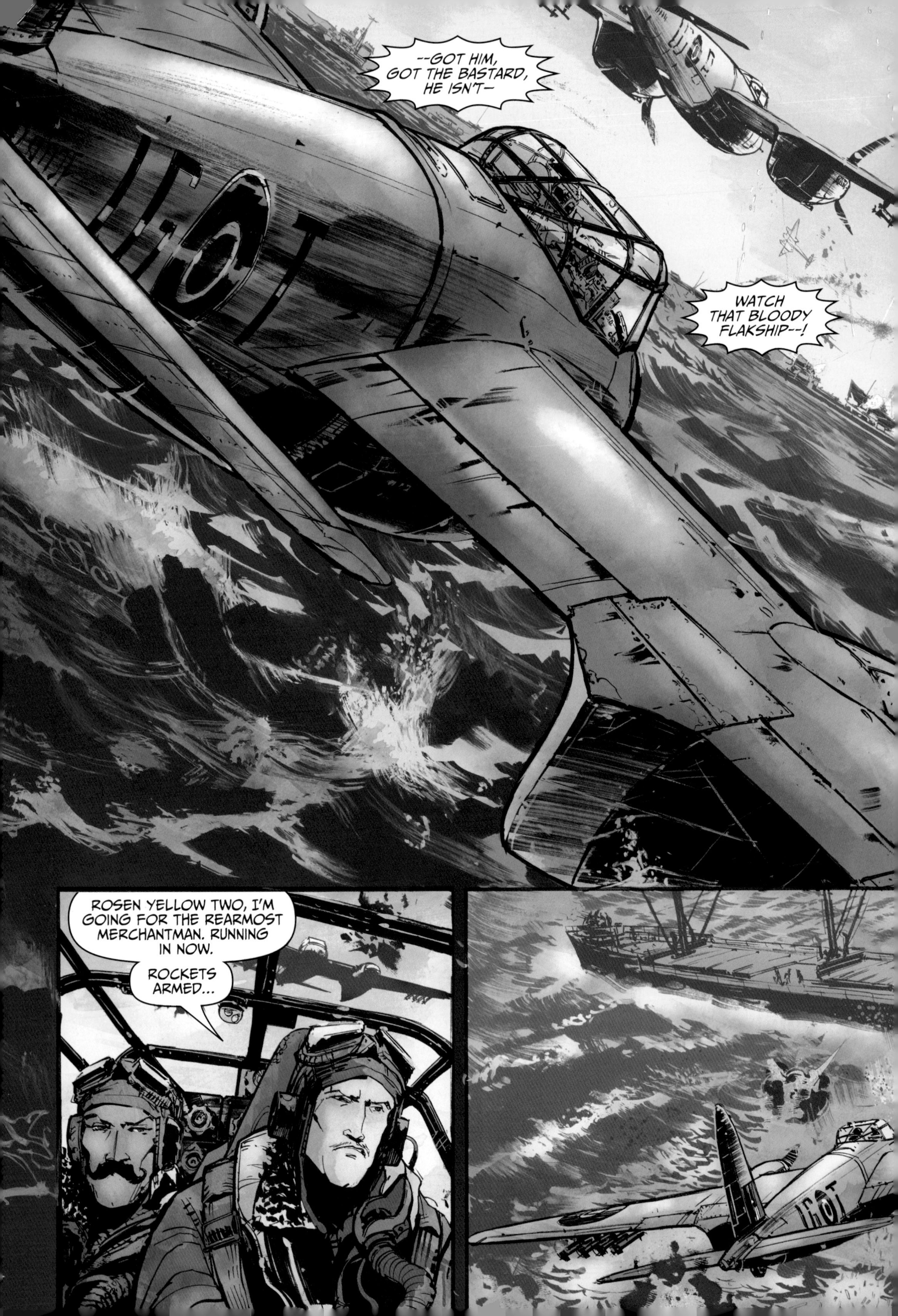
--GOT HIM, GOT THE BASTARD, HE ISN'T--
WATCH THAT BLOODY FLAKSHIP--!
ROSEN YELLOW TWO, I'M GOING FOR THE REARMOST MERCHANTMAN. RUNNING IN NOW.
ROCKETS ARMED...

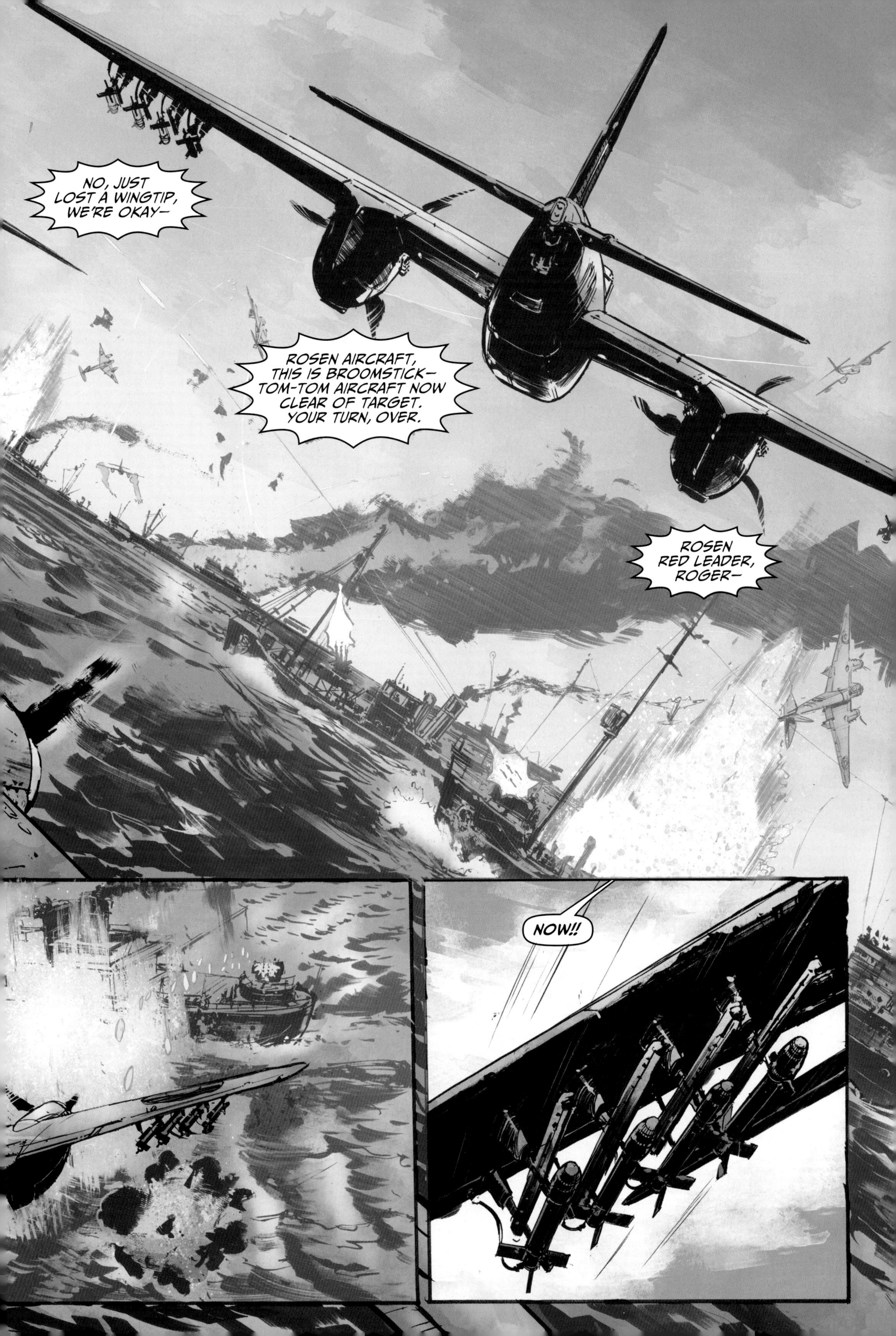
NO, JUST LOST A WINGTIP, WE'RE OKAY—
ROSEN AIRCRAFT, THIS IS BROOMSTICK—TOM-TOM AIRCRAFT NOW CLEAR OF TARGET. YOUR TURN, OVER.
ROSEN RED LEADER, ROGER—
NOW!!

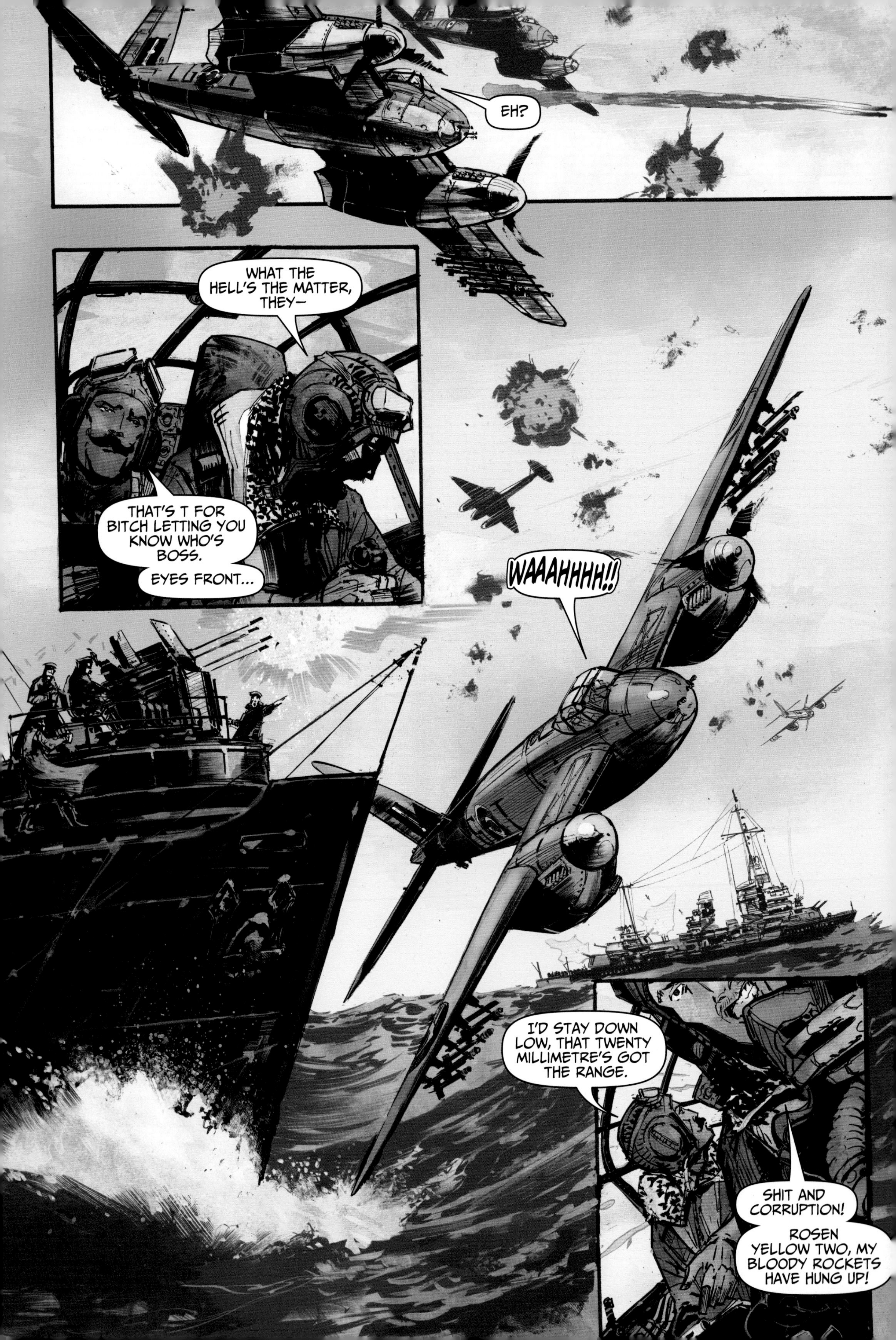
EH?
WHAT THE HELL'S THE MATTER, THEY–
THAT'S T FOR BITCH LETTING YOU KNOW WHO'S BOSS.
EYES FRONT...
WAAAHHHH!!
I'D STAY DOWN LOW, THAT TWENTY MILLIMETRE'S GOT THE RANGE.
SHIT AND CORRUPTION!
ROSEN YELLOW TWO, MY BLOODY ROCKETS HAVE HUNG UP!

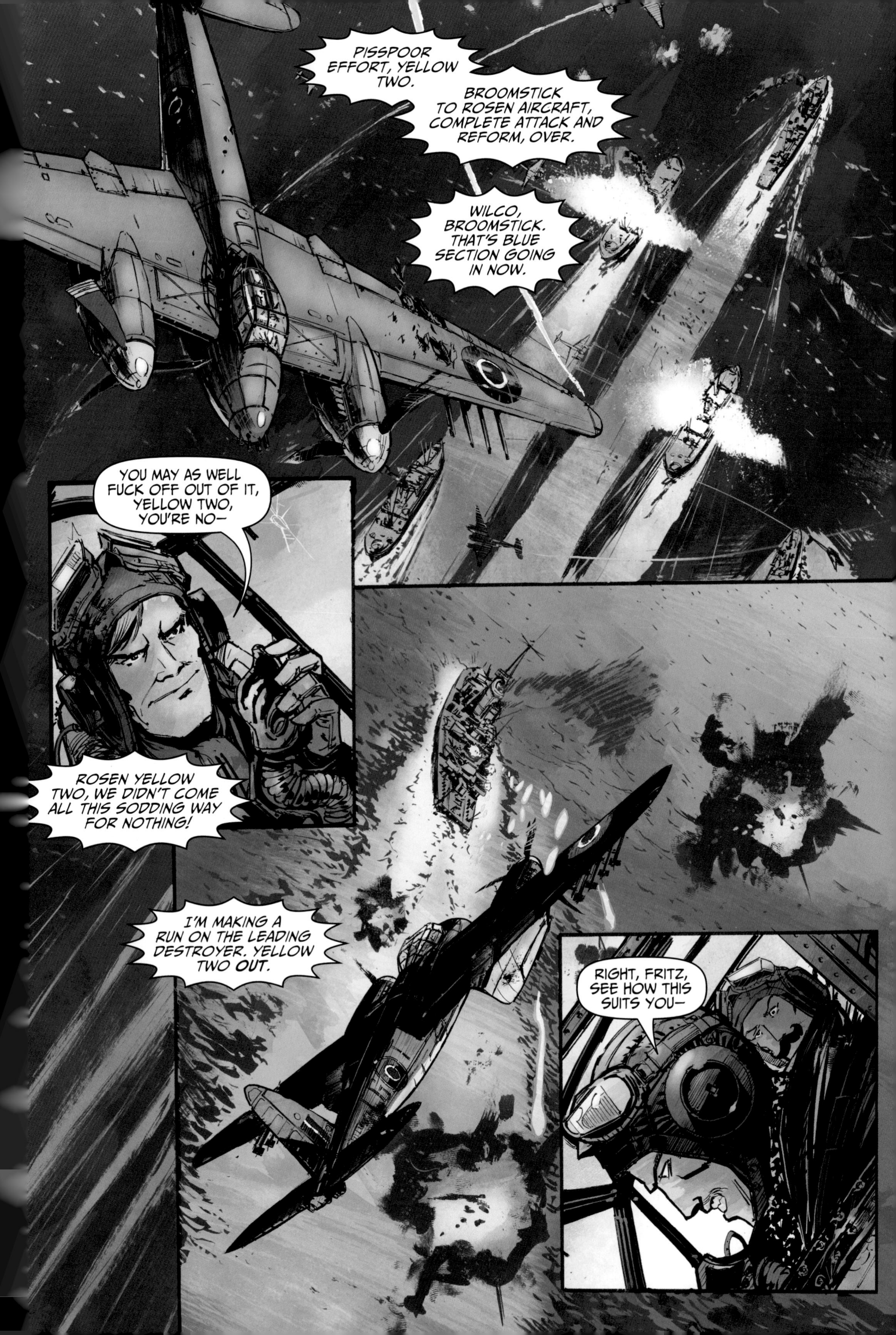
PISSPOOR EFFORT, YELLOW TWO.
BROOMSTICK TO ROSEN AIRCRAFT, COMPLETE ATTACK AND REFORM, OVER.
WILCO, BROOMSTICK. THAT'S BLUE SECTION GOING IN NOW.
YOU MAY AS WELL FUCK OFF OUT OF IT, YELLOW TWO, YOU'RE NO–
ROSEN YELLOW TWO, WE DIDN'T COME ALL THIS SODDING WAY FOR NOTHING!
I'M MAKING A RUN ON THE LEADING DESTROYER. YELLOW TWO OUT.
RIGHT, FRITZ, SEE HOW THIS SUITS YOU–

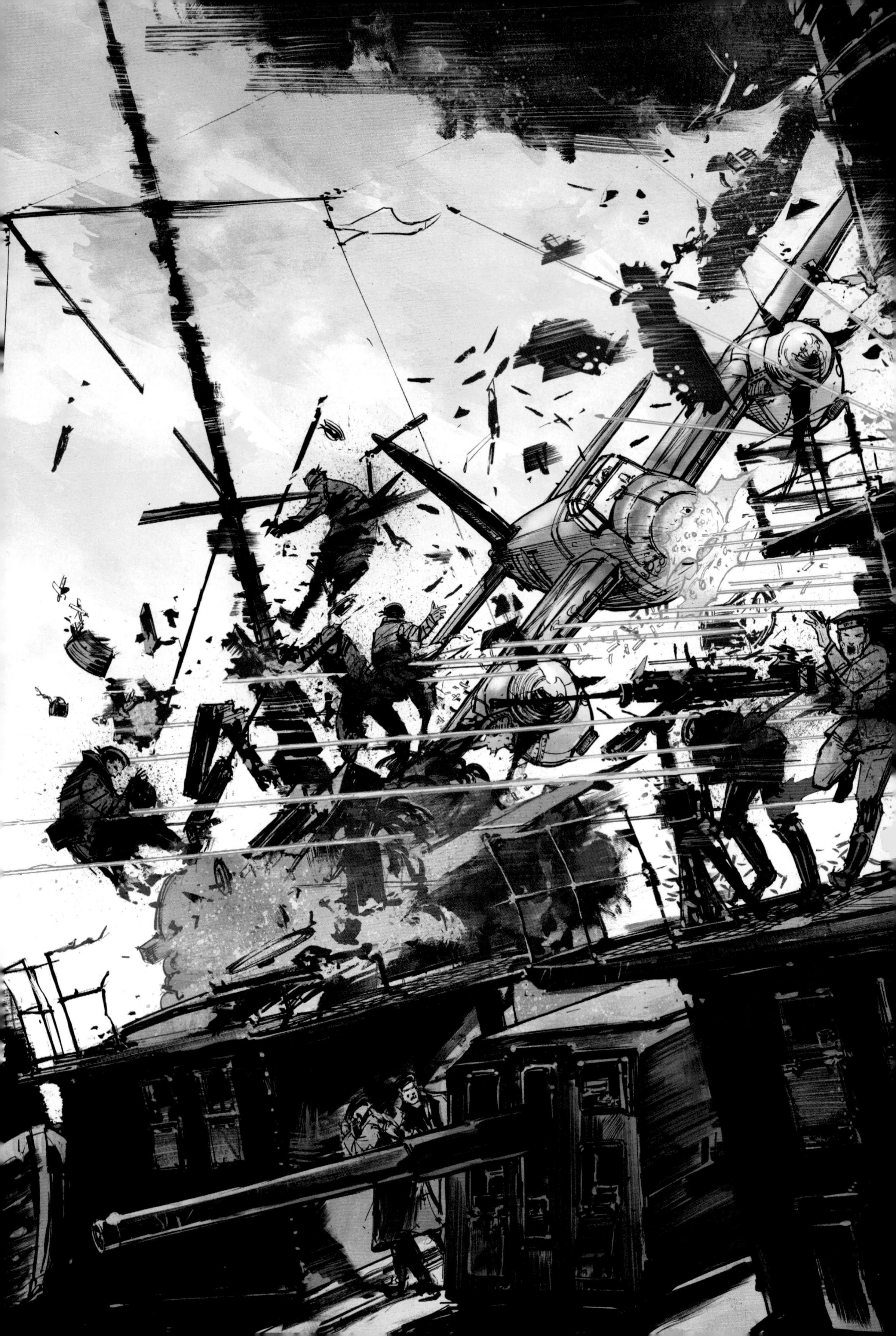

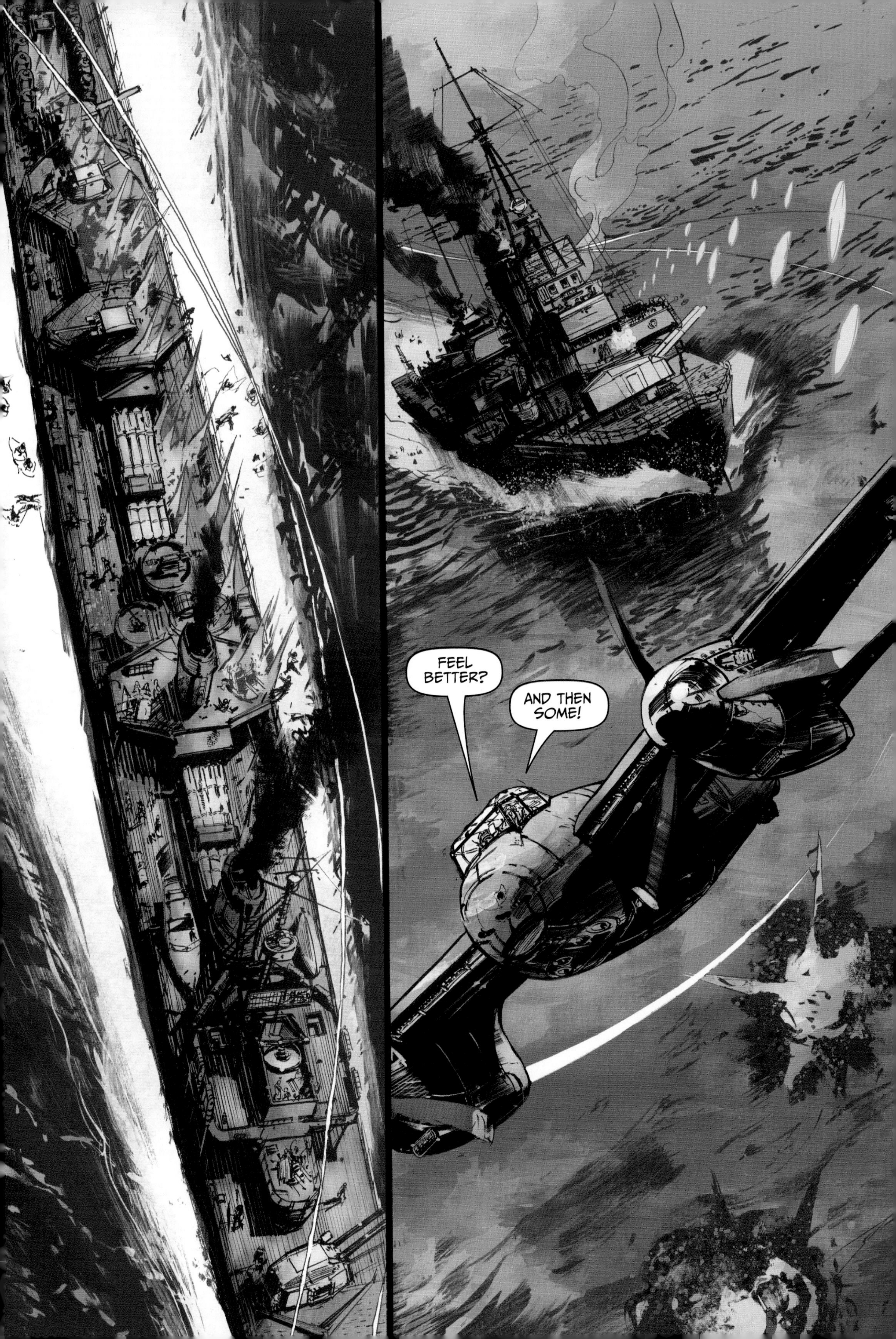
FEEL BETTER?
AND THEN SOME!

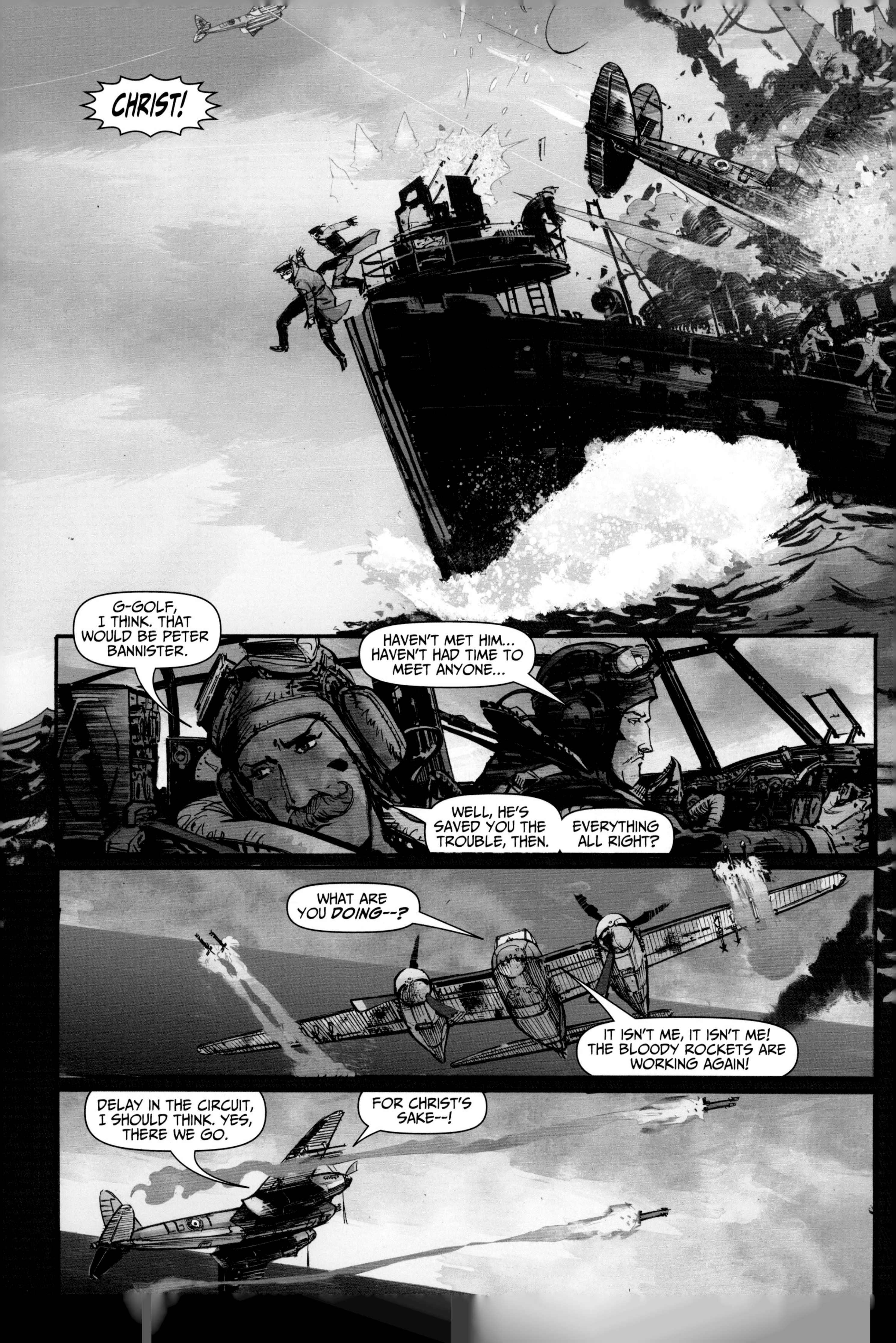
CHRIST!
G-GOLF, I THINK. THAT WOULD BE PETER BANNISTER.
HAVEN'T MET HIM... HAVEN'T HAD TIME TO MEET ANYONE...
WELL, HE'S SAVED YOU THE TROUBLE, THEN.
EVERYTHING ALL RIGHT?
WHAT ARE YOU *DOING*--?
IT ISN'T ME, IT ISN'T ME! THE BLOODY ROCKETS ARE WORKING AGAIN!
DELAY IN THE CIRCUIT, I SHOULD THINK. YES, THERE WE GO.
FOR CHRIST'S SAKE--!

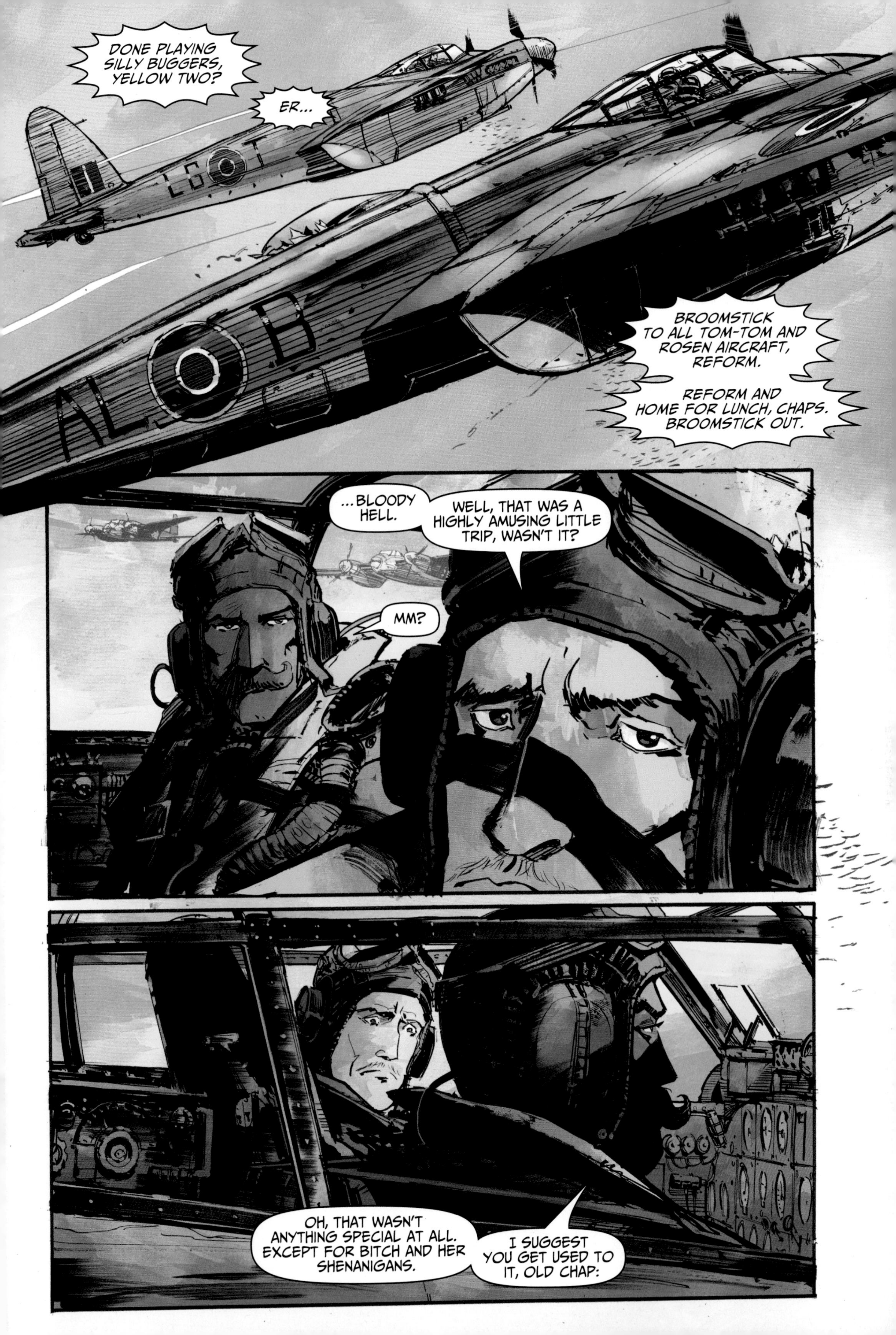
DONE PLAYING SILLY BUGGERS, YELLOW TWO?
ER...
BROOMSTICK TO ALL TOM-TOM AND ROSEN AIRCRAFT, REFORM.
REFORM AND HOME FOR LUNCH, CHAPS. BROOMSTICK OUT.
...BLOODY HELL.
WELL, THAT WAS A HIGHLY AMUSING LITTLE TRIP, WASN'T IT?
MM?
OH, THAT WASN'T ANYTHING SPECIAL AT ALL. EXCEPT FOR BITCH AND HER SHENANIGANS.
I SUGGEST YOU GET USED TO IT, OLD CHAP:

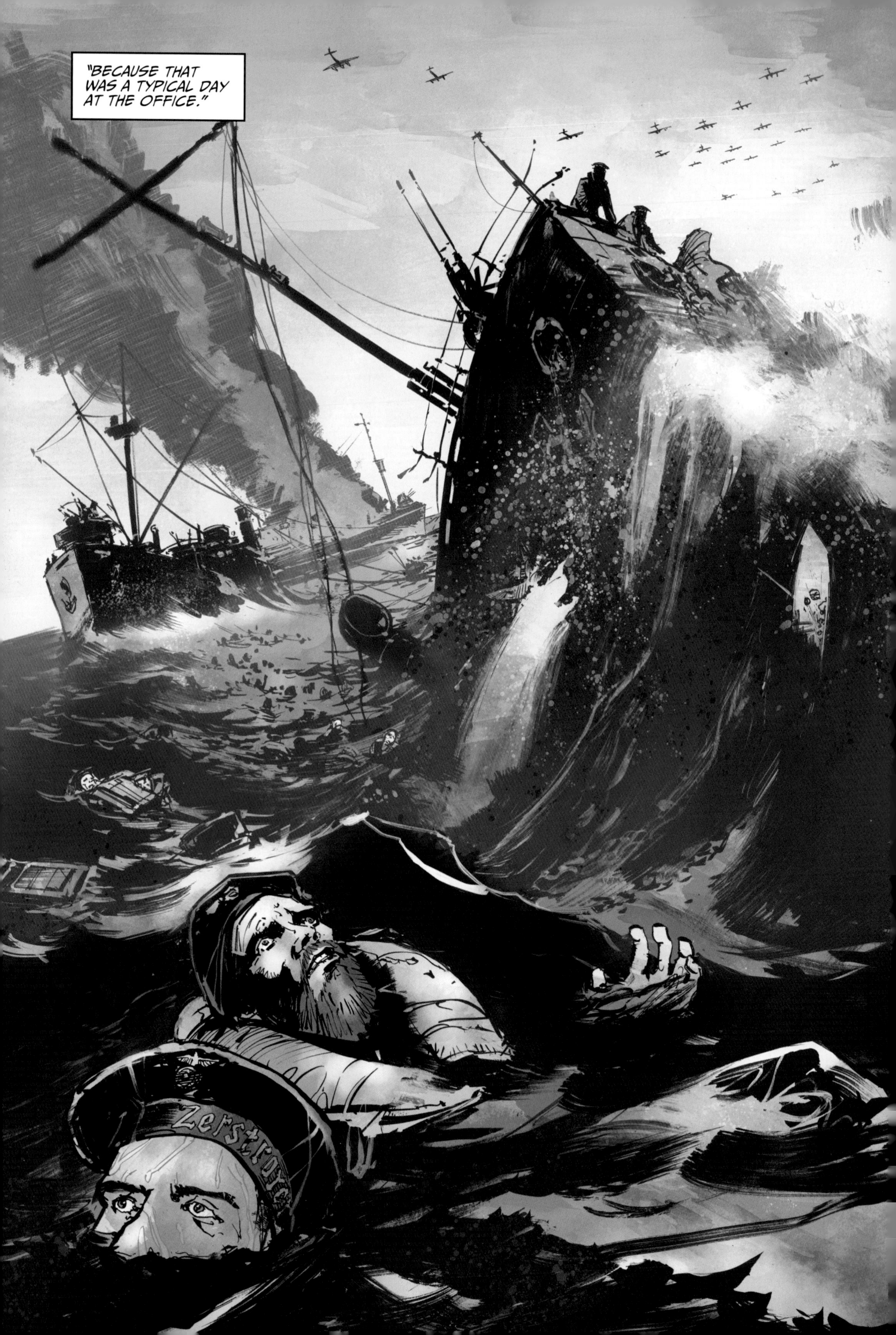
"BECAUSE THAT WAS A TYPICAL DAY AT THE OFFICE."

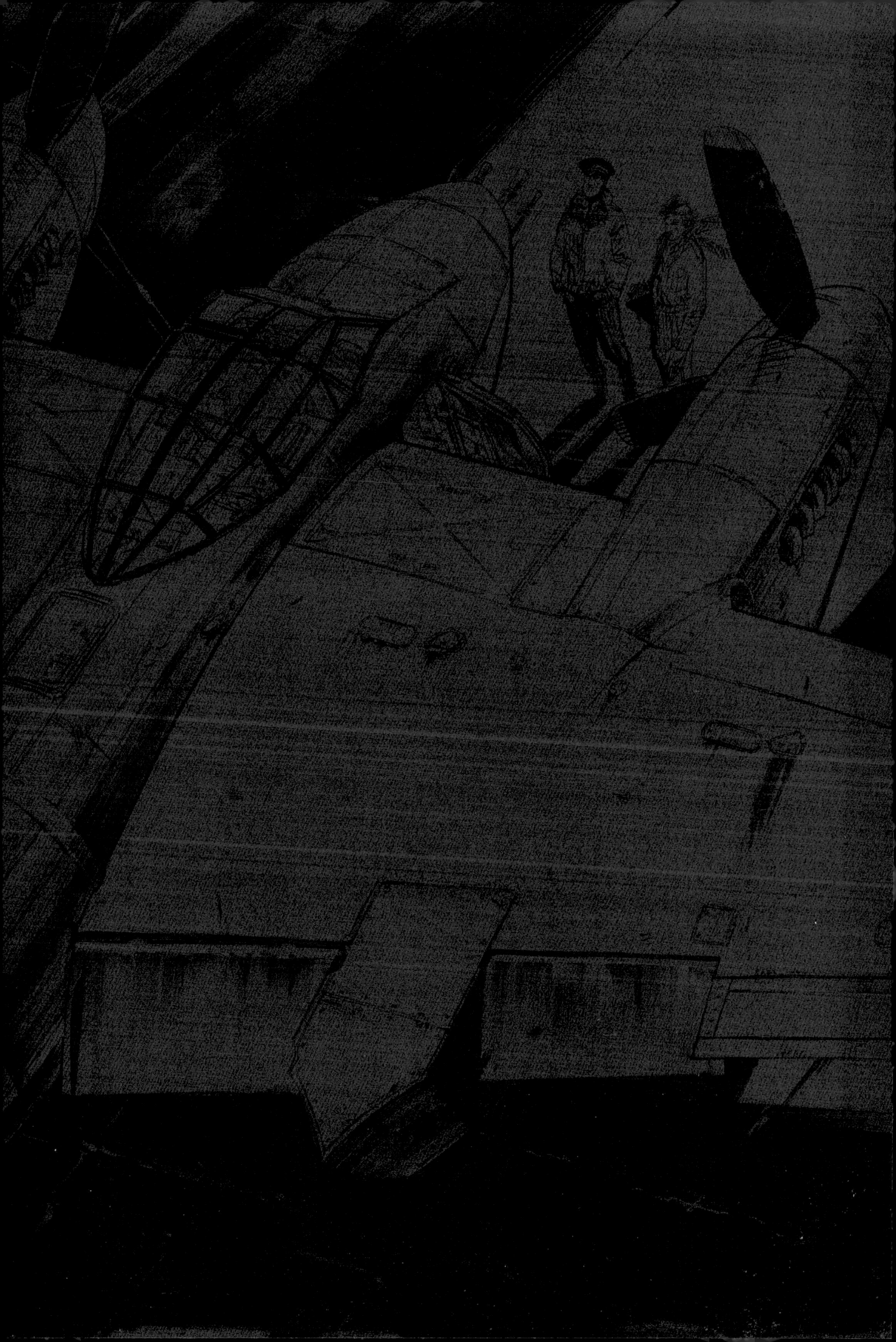

2: WARS WITHIN WARS

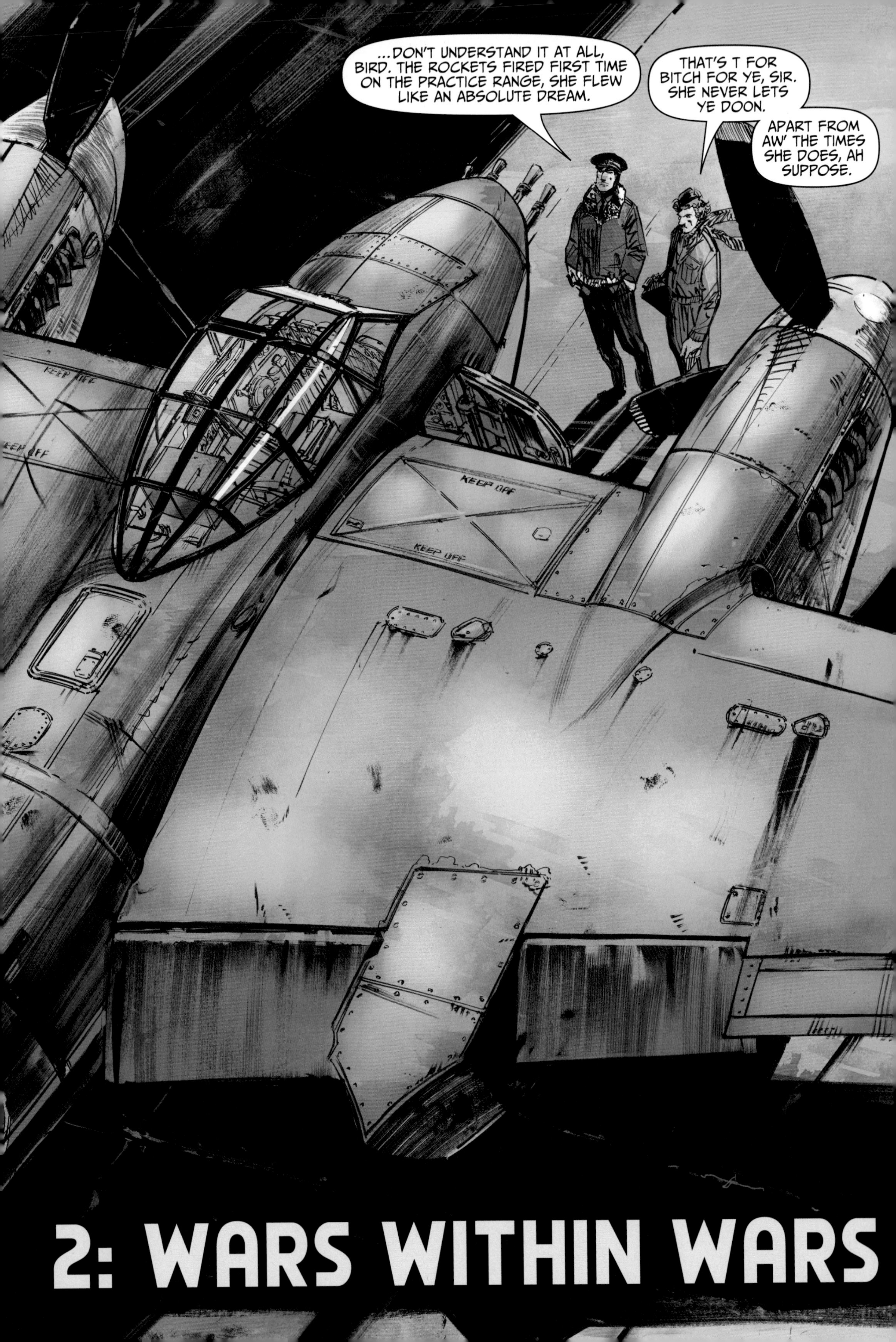
...DON'T UNDERSTAND IT AT ALL, BIRD. THE ROCKETS FIRED FIRST TIME ON THE PRACTICE RANGE, SHE FLEW LIKE AN ABSOLUTE DREAM.
THAT'S T FOR BITCH FOR YE, SIR. SHE NEVER LETS YE DOON.
APART FROM AW' THE TIMES SHE DOES, AH SUPPOSE.
KEEP OFF
KEEP OFF
KEEP OFF
KEEP OFF

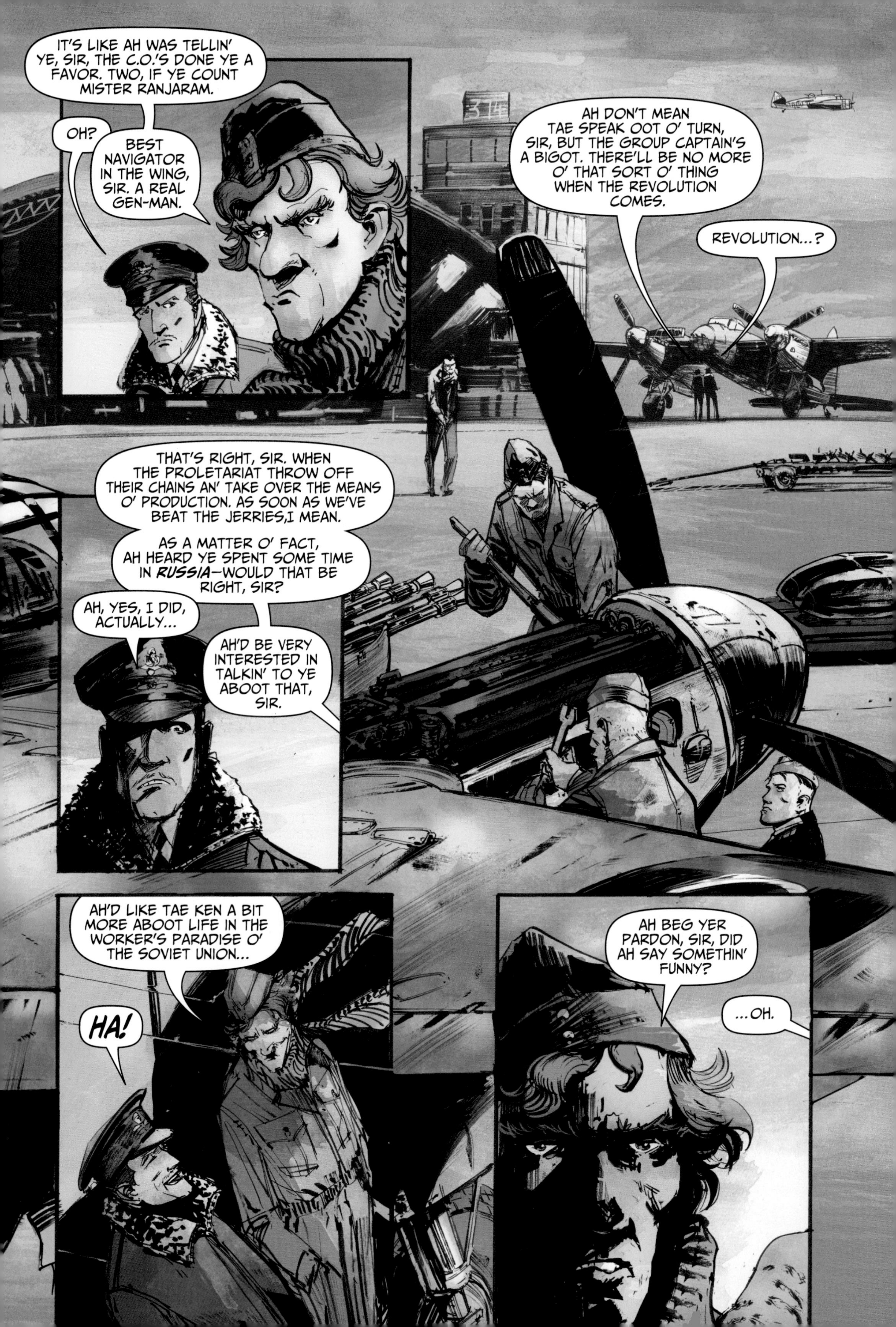
IT'S LIKE AH WAS TELLIN' YE, SIR, THE C.O.'S DONE YE A FAVOR. TWO, IF YE COUNT MISTER RANJARAM.
OH?
BEST NAVIGATOR IN THE WING, SIR. A REAL GEN-MAN.
AH DON'T MEAN TAE SPEAK OOT O' TURN, SIR, BUT THE GROUP CAPTAIN'S A BIGOT. THERE'LL BE NO MORE O' THAT SORT O' THING WHEN THE REVOLUTION COMES.
REVOLUTION...?
THAT'S RIGHT, SIR. WHEN THE PROLETARIAT THROW OFF THEIR CHAINS AN' TAKE OVER THE MEANS O' PRODUCTION. AS SOON AS WE'VE BEAT THE JERRIES,I MEAN.
AS A MATTER O' FACT, AH HEARD YE SPENT SOME TIME IN *RUSSIA*—WOULD THAT BE RIGHT, SIR?
AH, YES, I DID, ACTUALLY...
AH'D BE VERY INTERESTED IN TALKIN' TO YE ABOOT THAT, SIR.
AH'D LIKE TAE KEN A BIT MORE ABOOT LIFE IN THE WORKER'S PARADISE O' THE SOVIET UNION...
HA!
AH BEG YER PARDON, SIR, DID AH SAY SOMETHIN' FUNNY?
...OH.

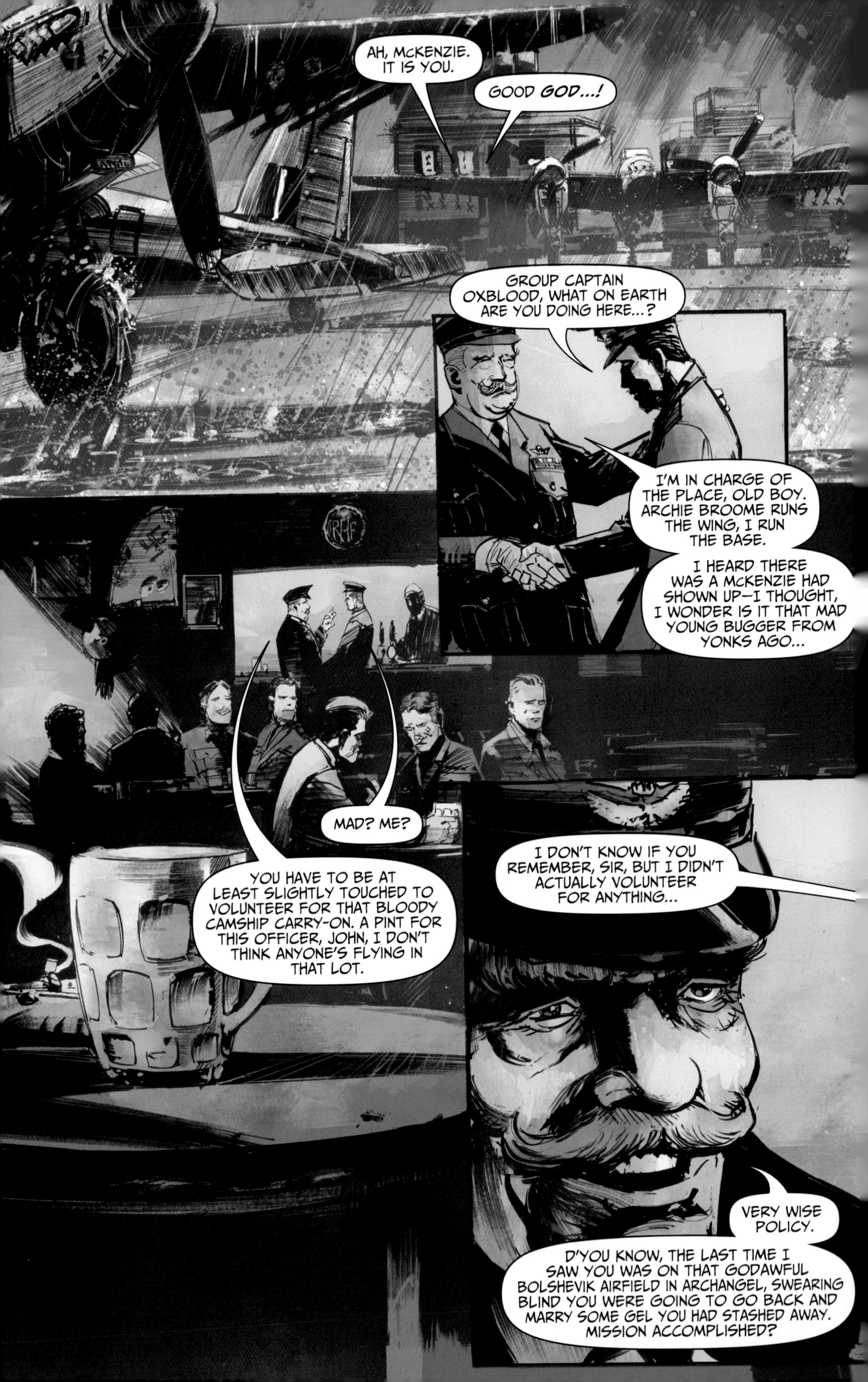
AH, MCKENZIE. IT IS YOU.
GOOD GOD...!
GROUP CAPTAIN OXBLOOD, WHAT ON EARTH ARE YOU DOING HERE...?
I'M IN CHARGE OF THE PLACE, OLD BOY. ARCHIE BROOME RUNS THE WING, I RUN THE BASE.
I HEARD THERE WAS A MCKENZIE HAD SHOWN UP—I THOUGHT, I WONDER IS IT THAT MAD YOUNG BUGGER FROM YONKS AGO...
MAD? ME?
YOU HAVE TO BE AT LEAST SLIGHTLY TOUCHED TO VOLUNTEER FOR THAT BLOODY CAMSHIP CARRY-ON. A PINT FOR THIS OFFICER, JOHN, I DON'T THINK ANYONE'S FLYING IN THAT LOT.
I DON'T KNOW IF YOU REMEMBER, SIR, BUT I DIDN'T ACTUALLY VOLUNTEER FOR ANYTHING...
VERY WISE POLICY.
D'YOU KNOW, THE LAST TIME I SAW YOU WAS ON THAT GODAWFUL BOLSHEVIK AIRFIELD IN ARCHANGEL, SWEARING BLIND YOU WERE GOING TO GO BACK AND MARRY SOME GEL YOU HAD STASHED AWAY. MISSION ACCOMPLISHED?

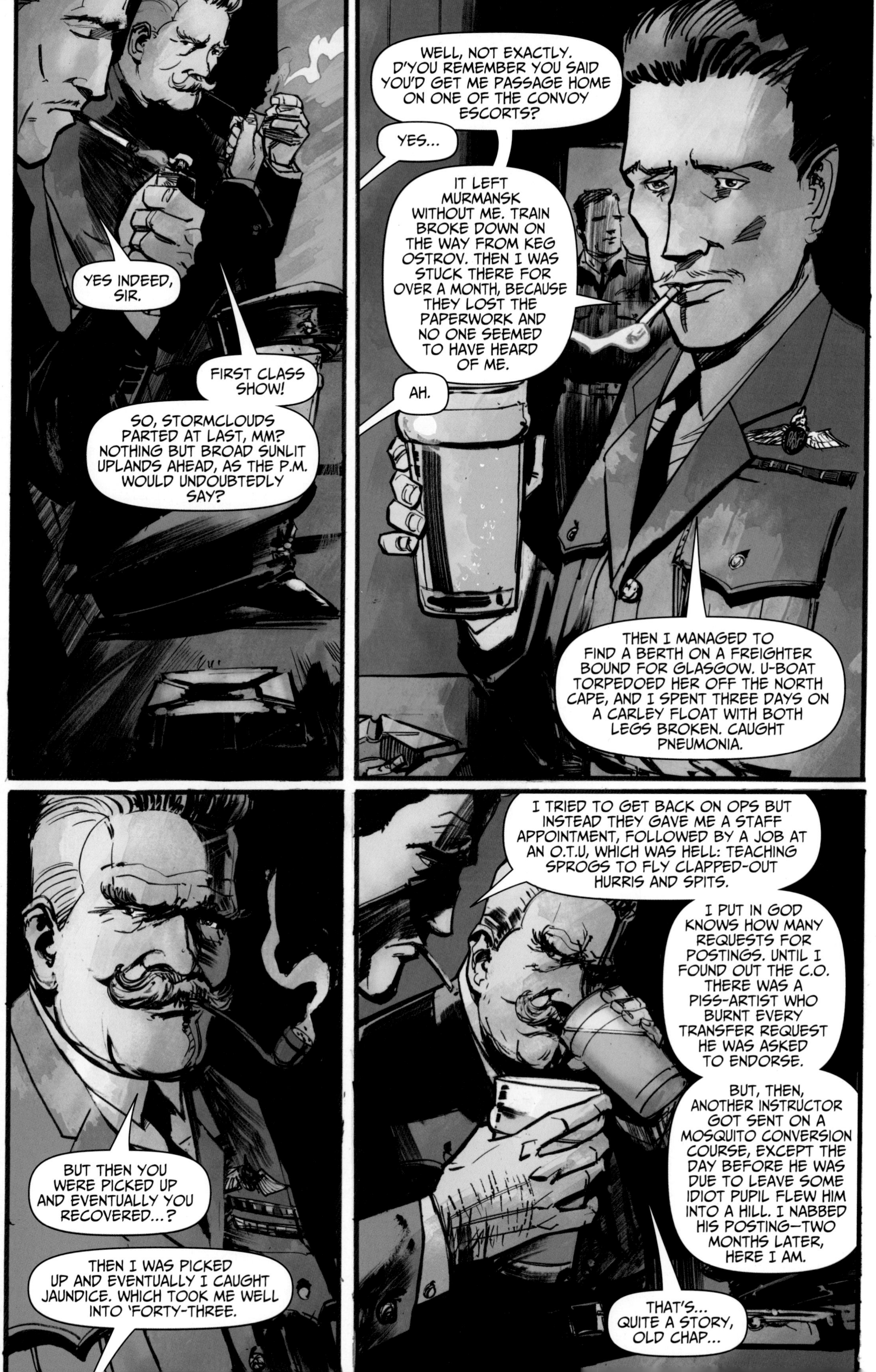
YES INDEED, SIR.
FIRST CLASS SHOW!
SO, STORMCLOUDS PARTED AT LAST, MM? NOTHING BUT BROAD SUNLIT UPLANDS AHEAD, AS THE P.M. WOULD UNDOUBTEDLY SAY?
WELL, NOT EXACTLY. D'YOU REMEMBER YOU SAID YOU'D GET ME PASSAGE HOME ON ONE OF THE CONVOY ESCORTS?
YES...
IT LEFT MURMANSK WITHOUT ME. TRAIN BROKE DOWN ON THE WAY FROM KEG OSTROV. THEN I WAS STUCK THERE FOR OVER A MONTH, BECAUSE THEY LOST THE PAPERWORK AND NO ONE SEEMED TO HAVE HEARD OF ME.
AH.
THEN I MANAGED TO FIND A BERTH ON A FREIGHTER BOUND FOR GLASGOW. U-BOAT TORPEDOED HER OFF THE NORTH CAPE, AND I SPENT THREE DAYS ON A CARLEY FLOAT WITH BOTH LEGS BROKEN. CAUGHT PNEUMONIA.
BUT THEN YOU WERE PICKED UP AND EVENTUALLY YOU RECOVERED...?
THEN I WAS PICKED UP AND EVENTUALLY I CAUGHT JAUNDICE. WHICH TOOK ME WELL INTO 'FORTY-THREE.
I TRIED TO GET BACK ON OPS BUT INSTEAD THEY GAVE ME A STAFF APPOINTMENT, FOLLOWED BY A JOB AT AN O.T.U, WHICH WAS HELL: TEACHING SPROGS TO FLY CLAPPED-OUT HURRIS AND SPITS.
I PUT IN GOD KNOWS HOW MANY REQUESTS FOR POSTINGS. UNTIL I FOUND OUT THE C.O. THERE WAS A PISS-ARTIST WHO BURNT EVERY TRANSFER REQUEST HE WAS ASKED TO ENDORSE.
BUT, THEN, ANOTHER INSTRUCTOR GOT SENT ON A MOSQUITO CONVERSION COURSE, EXCEPT THE DAY BEFORE HE WAS DUE TO LEAVE SOME IDIOT PUPIL FLEW HIM INTO A HILL. I NABBED HIS POSTING—TWO MONTHS LATER, HERE I AM.
THAT'S... QUITE A STORY, OLD CHAP...

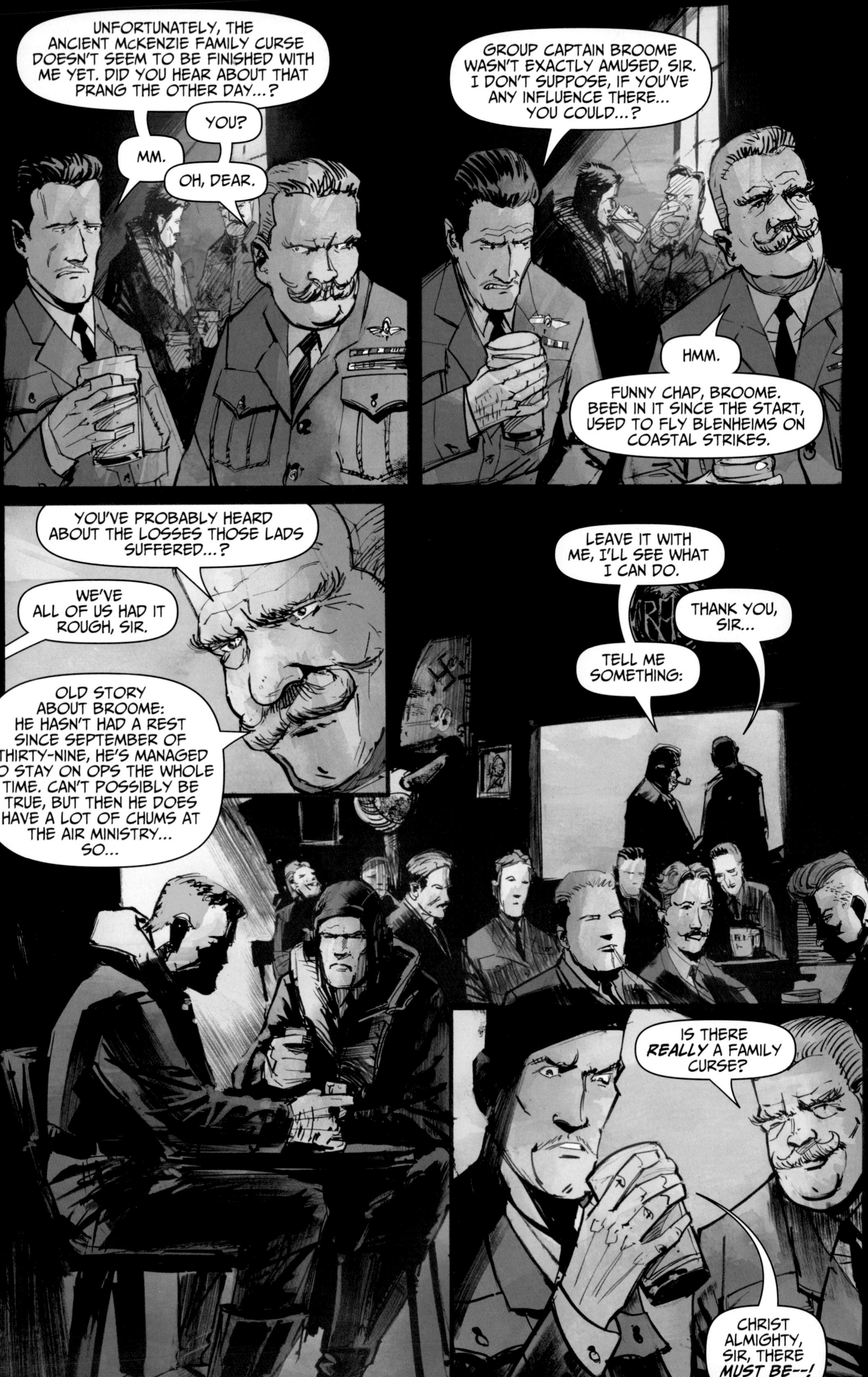
UNFORTUNATELY, THE ANCIENT McKENZIE FAMILY CURSE DOESN'T SEEM TO BE FINISHED WITH ME YET. DID YOU HEAR ABOUT THAT PRANG THE OTHER DAY...?
YOU?
MM.
OH, DEAR.
GROUP CAPTAIN BROOME WASN'T EXACTLY AMUSED, SIR. I DON'T SUPPOSE, IF YOU'VE ANY INFLUENCE THERE... YOU COULD...?
HMM.
FUNNY CHAP, BROOME. BEEN IN IT SINCE THE START, USED TO FLY BLENHEIMS ON COASTAL STRIKES.
YOU'VE PROBABLY HEARD ABOUT THE LOSSES THOSE LADS SUFFERED...?
WE'VE ALL OF US HAD IT ROUGH, SIR.
OLD STORY ABOUT BROOME: HE HASN'T HAD A REST SINCE SEPTEMBER OF 'THIRTY-NINE, HE'S MANAGED TO STAY ON OPS THE WHOLE TIME. CAN'T POSSIBLY BE TRUE, BUT THEN HE DOES HAVE A LOT OF CHUMS AT THE AIR MINISTRY... SO...
LEAVE IT WITH ME, I'LL SEE WHAT I CAN DO.
THANK YOU, SIR...
TELL ME SOMETHING:
IS THERE *REALLY* A FAMILY CURSE?
CHRIST ALMIGHTY, SIR, THERE *MUST BE*--!

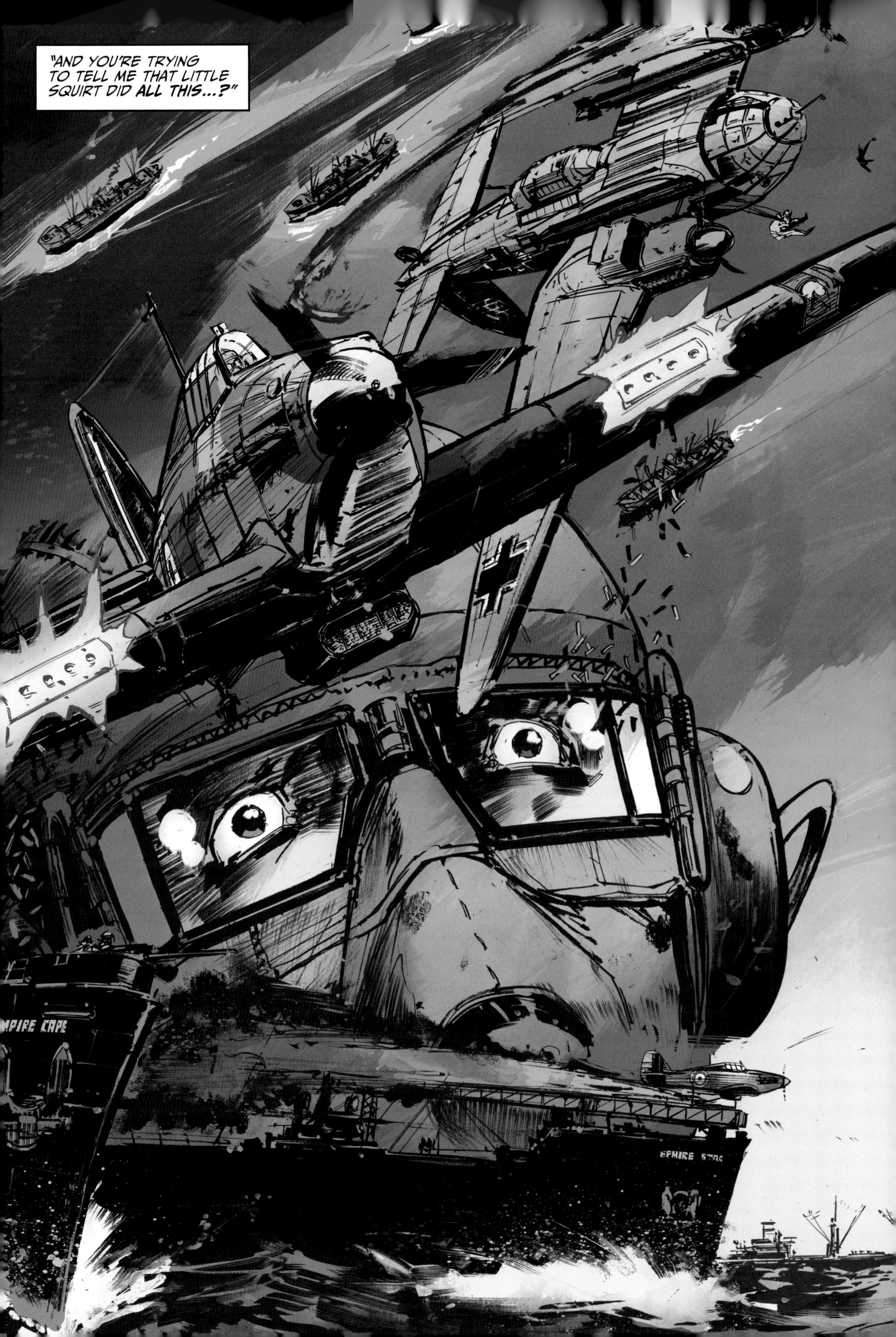
"AND YOU'RE TRYING TO TELL ME THAT LITTLE SQUIRT DID **ALL THIS...?**"

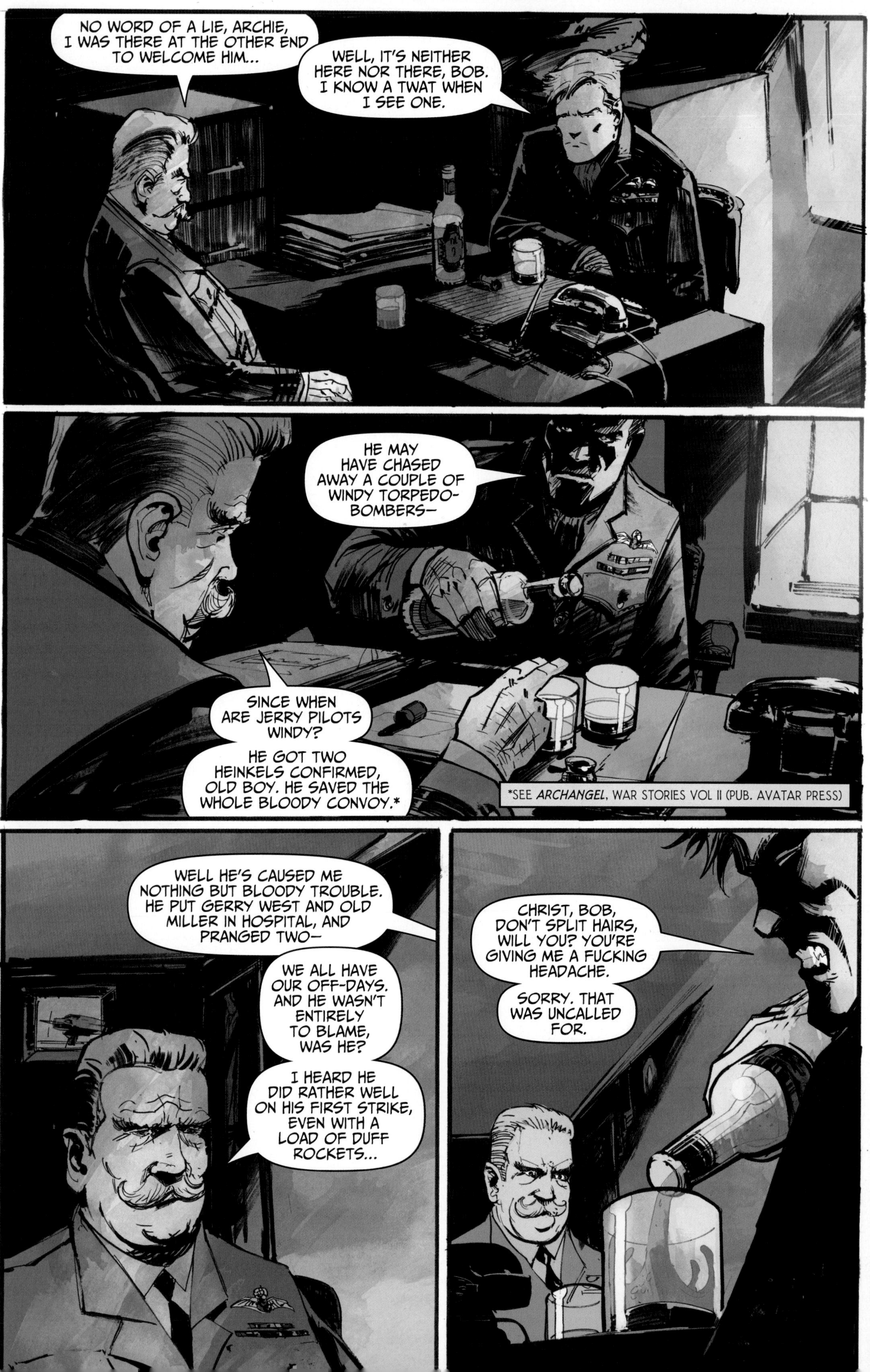

NO WORD OF A LIE, ARCHIE, I WAS THERE AT THE OTHER END TO WELCOME HIM...
WELL, IT'S NEITHER HERE NOR THERE, BOB. I KNOW A TWAT WHEN I SEE ONE.
HE MAY HAVE CHASED AWAY A COUPLE OF WINDY TORPEDO-BOMBERS—
SINCE WHEN ARE JERRY PILOTS WINDY?
HE GOT TWO HEINKELS CONFIRMED, OLD BOY. HE SAVED THE WHOLE BLOODY CONVOY.*
*SEE ARCHANGEL, WAR STORIES VOL II (PUB. AVATAR PRESS)
WELL HE'S CAUSED ME NOTHING BUT BLOODY TROUBLE. HE PUT GERRY WEST AND OLD MILLER IN HOSPITAL, AND PRANGED TWO—
WE ALL HAVE OUR OFF-DAYS. AND HE WASN'T ENTIRELY TO BLAME, WAS HE?
I HEARD HE DID RATHER WELL ON HIS FIRST STRIKE, EVEN WITH A LOAD OF DUFF ROCKETS...
CHRIST, BOB, DON'T SPLIT HAIRS, WILL YOU? YOU'RE GIVING ME A FUCKING HEADACHE.
SORRY. THAT WAS UNCALLED FOR.

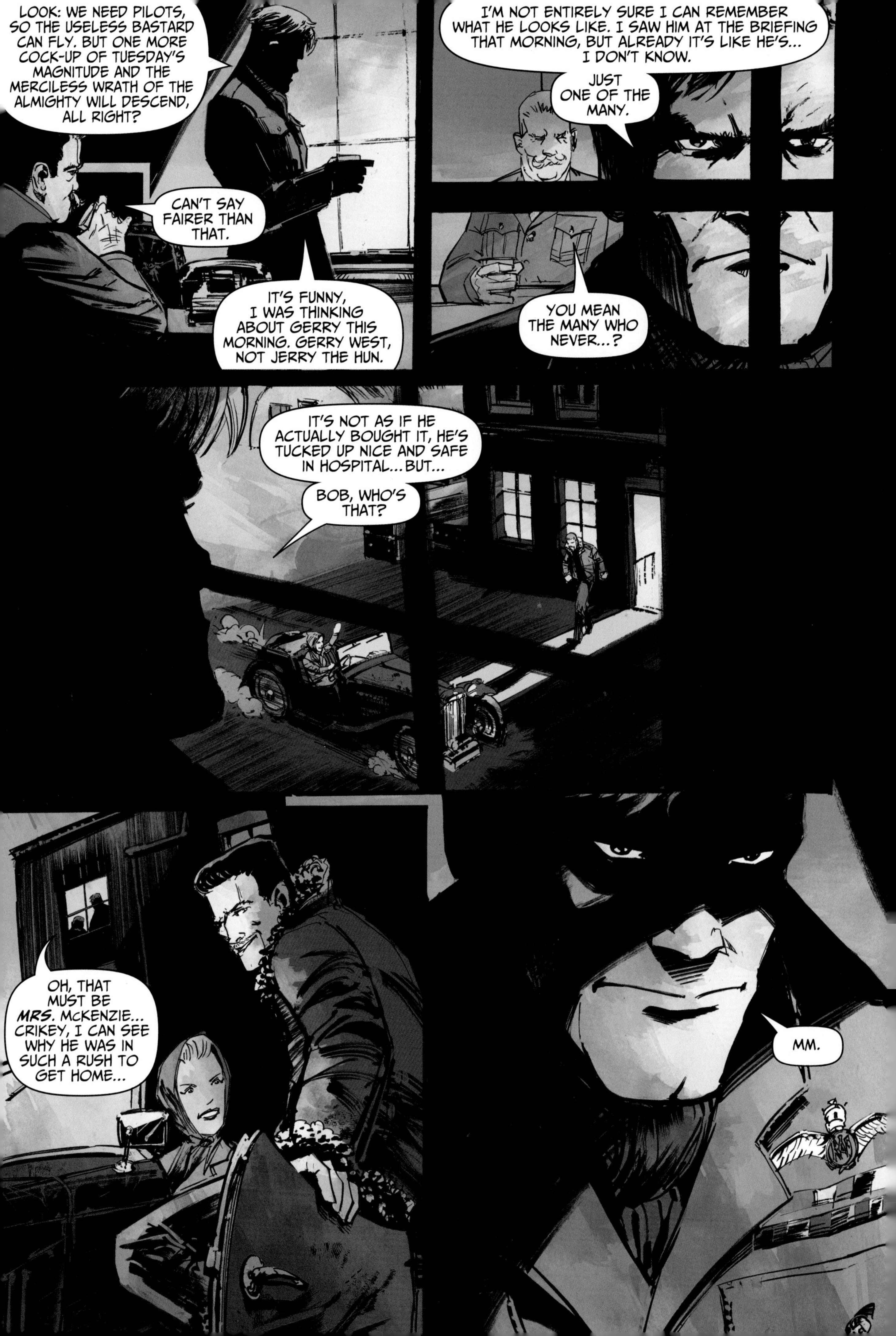
LOOK: WE NEED PILOTS, SO THE USELESS BASTARD CAN FLY. BUT ONE MORE COCK-UP OF TUESDAY'S MAGNITUDE AND THE MERCILESS WRATH OF THE ALMIGHTY WILL DESCEND, ALL RIGHT?
CAN'T SAY FAIRER THAN THAT.
IT'S FUNNY, I WAS THINKING ABOUT GERRY THIS MORNING. GERRY WEST, NOT JERRY THE HUN.
I'M NOT ENTIRELY SURE I CAN REMEMBER WHAT HE LOOKS LIKE. I SAW HIM AT THE BRIEFING THAT MORNING, BUT ALREADY IT'S LIKE HE'S... I DON'T KNOW.
JUST ONE OF THE MANY.
YOU MEAN THE MANY WHO NEVER...?
IT'S NOT AS IF HE ACTUALLY BOUGHT IT, HE'S TUCKED UP NICE AND SAFE IN HOSPITAL... BUT...
BOB, WHO'S THAT?
OH, THAT MUST BE ***MRS.*** McKENZIE... CRIKEY, I CAN SEE WHY HE WAS IN SUCH A RUSH TO GET HOME...
MM.

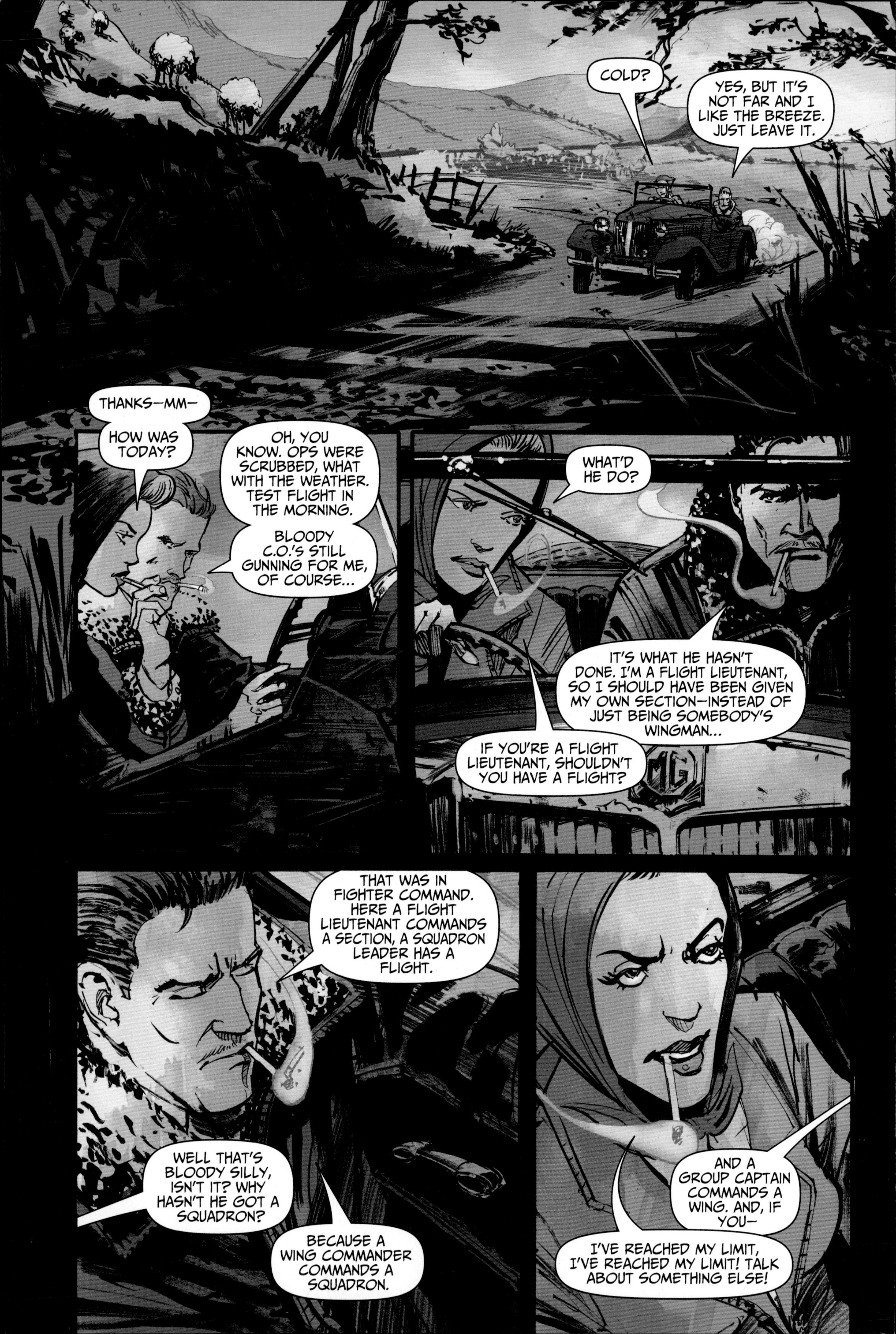
COLD?
YES, BUT IT'S NOT FAR AND I LIKE THE BREEZE. JUST LEAVE IT.
THANKS—MM—
HOW WAS TODAY?
OH, YOU KNOW. OPS WERE SCRUBBED, WHAT WITH THE WEATHER. TEST FLIGHT IN THE MORNING.
BLOODY C.O.'S STILL GUNNING FOR ME, OF COURSE...
WHAT'D HE DO?
IT'S WHAT HE HASN'T DONE. I'M A FLIGHT LIEUTENANT, SO I SHOULD HAVE BEEN GIVEN MY OWN SECTION—INSTEAD OF JUST BEING SOMEBODY'S WINGMAN...
IF YOU'RE A FLIGHT LIEUTENANT, SHOULDN'T YOU HAVE A FLIGHT?
MG
THAT WAS IN FIGHTER COMMAND. HERE A FLIGHT LIEUTENANT COMMANDS A SECTION, A SQUADRON LEADER HAS A FLIGHT.
WELL THAT'S BLOODY SILLY, ISN'T IT? WHY HASN'T HE GOT A SQUADRON?
BECAUSE A WING COMMANDER COMMANDS A SQUADRON.
AND A GROUP CAPTAIN COMMANDS A WING. AND, IF YOU—
I'VE REACHED MY LIMIT, I'VE REACHED MY LIMIT! TALK ABOUT SOMETHING ELSE!

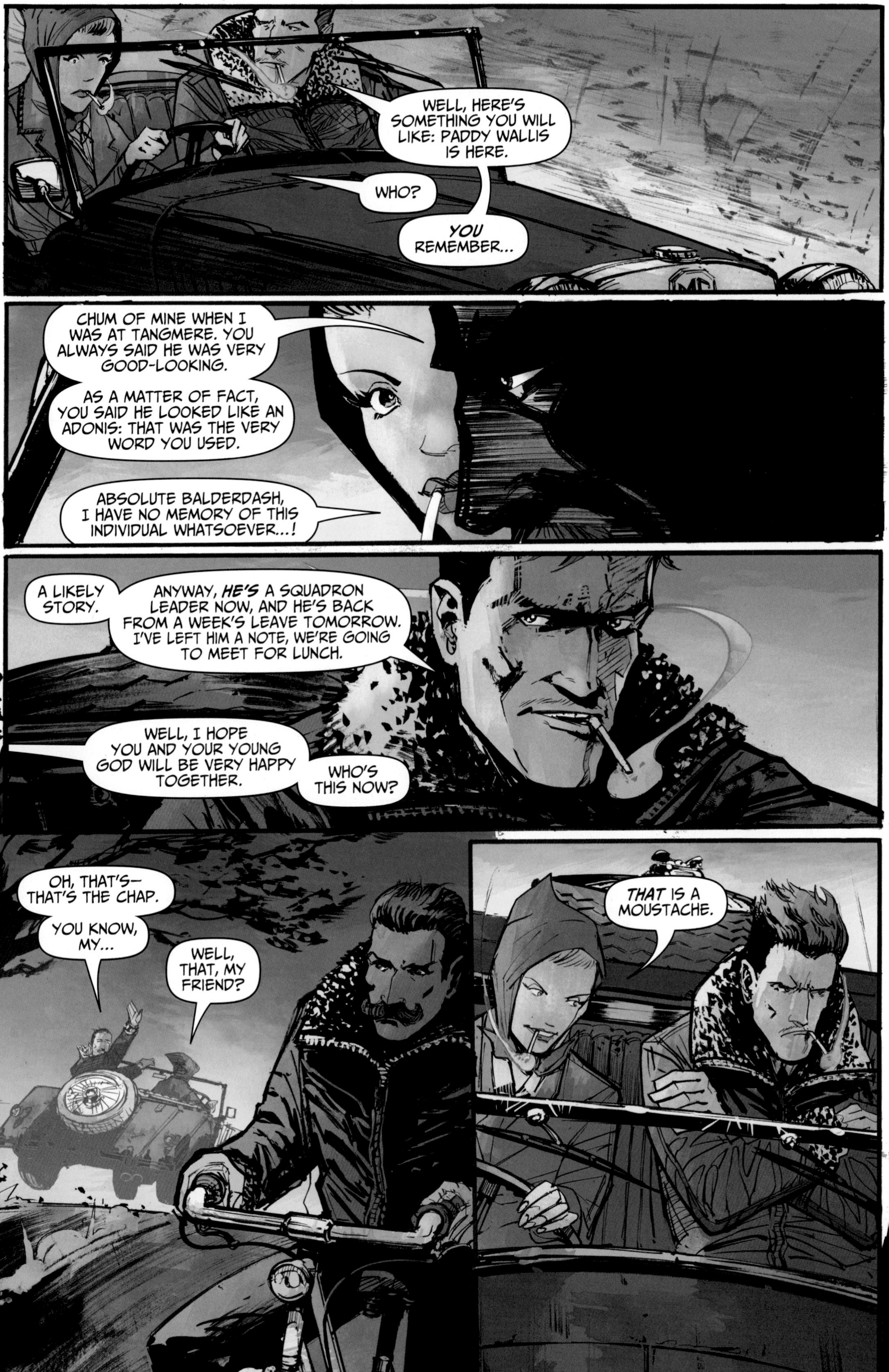
WELL, HERE'S SOMETHING YOU WILL LIKE: PADDY WALLIS IS HERE.
WHO?
YOU REMEMBER...
CHUM OF MINE WHEN I WAS AT TANGMERE. YOU ALWAYS SAID HE WAS VERY GOOD-LOOKING.
AS A MATTER OF FACT, YOU SAID HE LOOKED LIKE AN ADONIS: THAT WAS THE VERY WORD YOU USED.
ABSOLUTE BALDERDASH, I HAVE NO MEMORY OF THIS INDIVIDUAL WHATSOEVER...!
A LIKELY STORY.
ANYWAY, HE'S A SQUADRON LEADER NOW, AND HE'S BACK FROM A WEEK'S LEAVE TOMORROW. I'VE LEFT HIM A NOTE, WE'RE GOING TO MEET FOR LUNCH.
WELL, I HOPE YOU AND YOUR YOUNG GOD WILL BE VERY HAPPY TOGETHER.
WHO'S THIS NOW?
OH, THAT'S— THAT'S THE CHAP.
YOU KNOW, MY...
WELL, THAT, MY FRIEND?
THAT IS A MOUSTACHE.

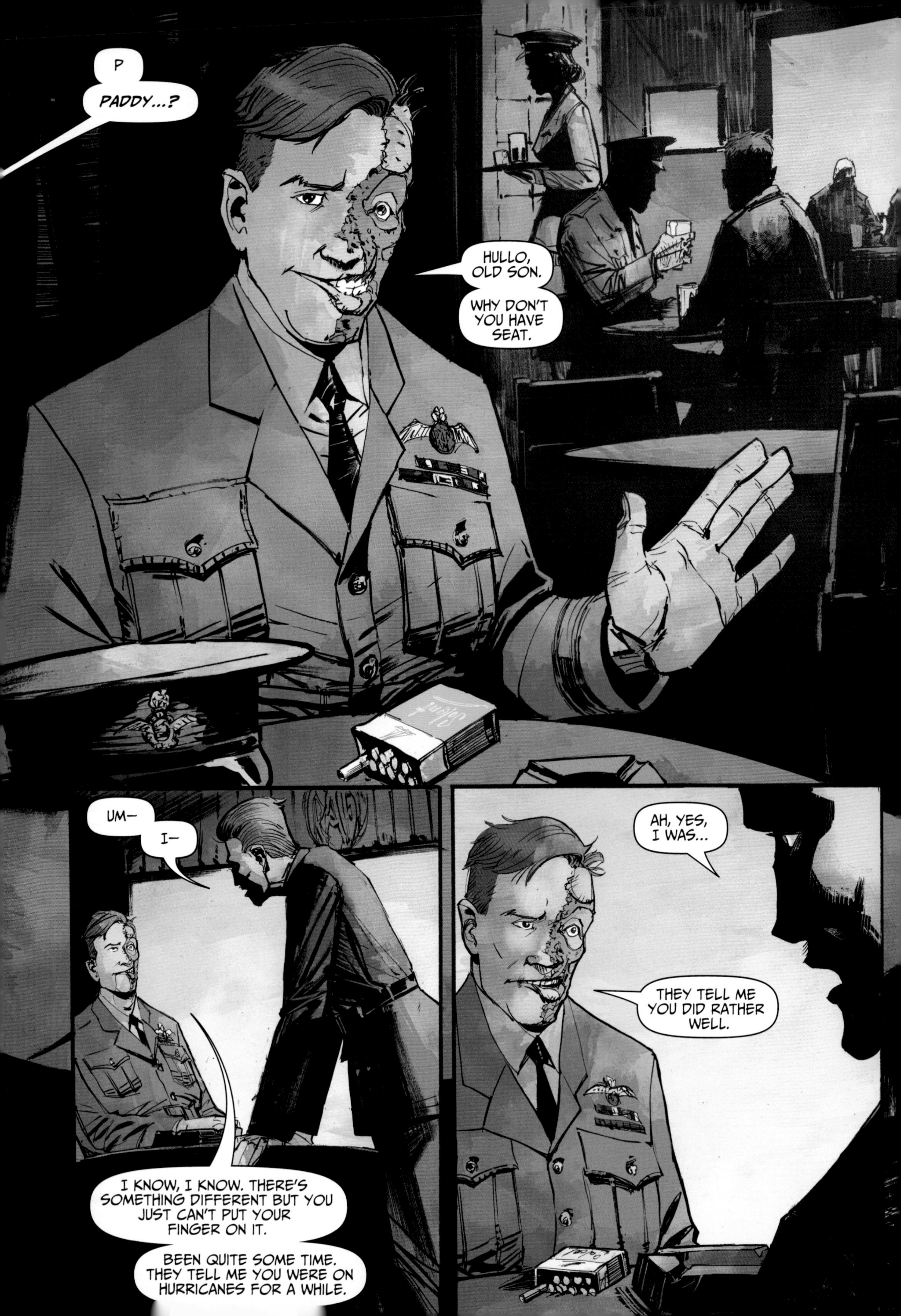
P
PADDY...?
HULLO, OLD SON.
WHY DON'T YOU HAVE SEAT.
UM—
I—
I KNOW, I KNOW. THERE'S SOMETHING DIFFERENT BUT YOU JUST CAN'T PUT YOUR FINGER ON IT.
BEEN QUITE SOME TIME. THEY TELL ME YOU WERE ON HURRICANES FOR A WHILE.
AH, YES, I WAS...
THEY TELL ME YOU DID RATHER WELL.

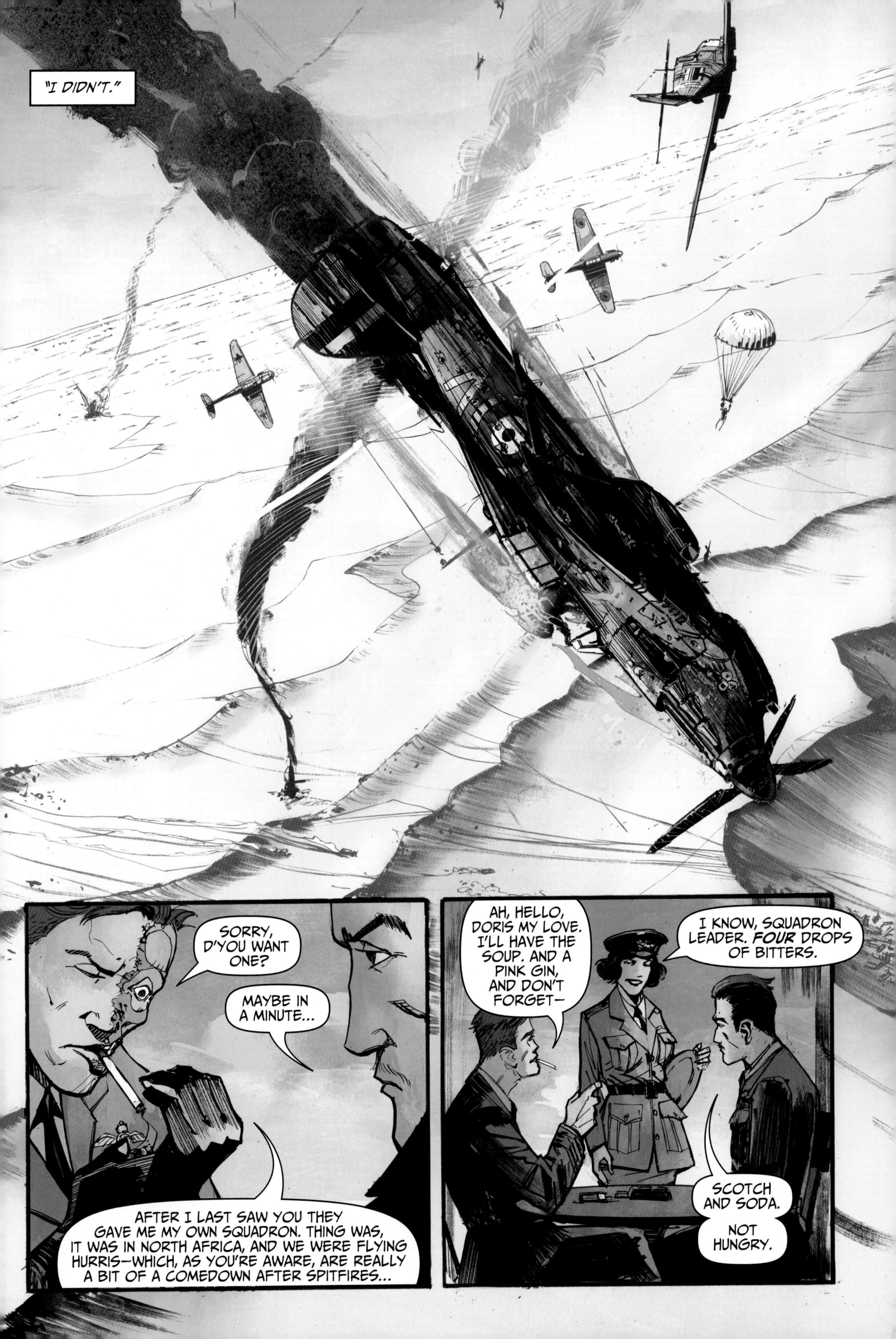
"I DIDN'T."
SORRY, D'YOU WANT ONE?
MAYBE IN A MINUTE...
AFTER I LAST SAW YOU THEY GAVE ME MY OWN SQUADRON. THING WAS, IT WAS IN NORTH AFRICA, AND WE WERE FLYING HURRIS—WHICH, AS YOU'RE AWARE, ARE REALLY A BIT OF A COMEDOWN AFTER SPITFIRES...
AH, HELLO, DORIS MY LOVE. I'LL HAVE THE SOUP. AND A PINK GIN, AND DON'T FORGET—
I KNOW, SQUADRON LEADER. ***FOUR*** DROPS OF BITTERS.
SCOTCH AND SODA.
NOT HUNGRY.

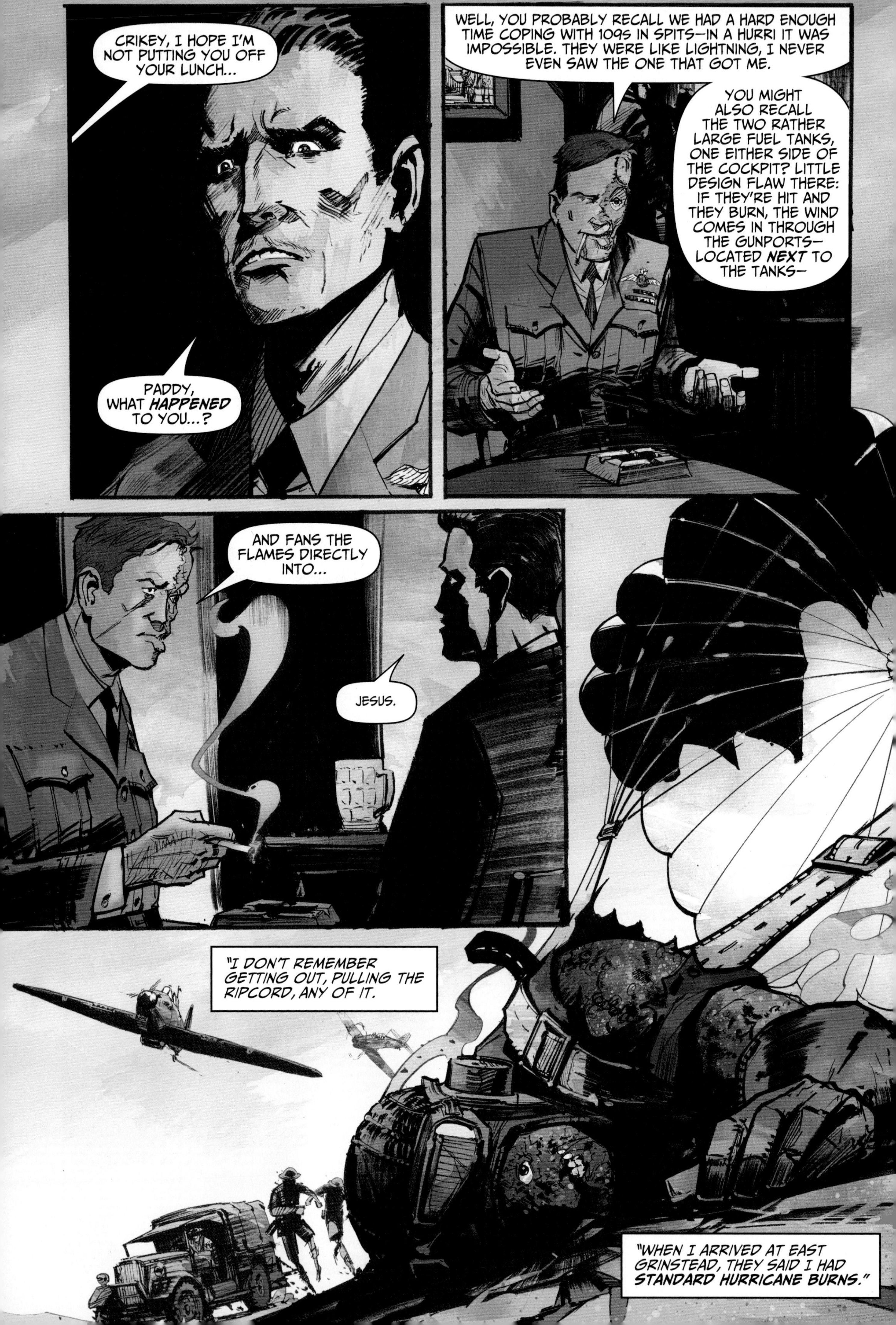
CRIKEY, I HOPE I'M NOT PUTTING YOU OFF YOUR LUNCH...
PADDY, WHAT **HAPPENED** TO YOU...?
WELL, YOU PROBABLY RECALL WE HAD A HARD ENOUGH TIME COPING WITH 109s IN SPITS—IN A HURRI IT WAS IMPOSSIBLE. THEY WERE LIKE LIGHTNING, I NEVER EVEN SAW THE ONE THAT GOT ME.
YOU MIGHT ALSO RECALL THE TWO RATHER LARGE FUEL TANKS, ONE EITHER SIDE OF THE COCKPIT? LITTLE DESIGN FLAW THERE: IF THEY'RE HIT AND THEY BURN, THE WIND COMES IN THROUGH THE GUNPORTS—LOCATED **NEXT** TO THE TANKS—
AND FANS THE FLAMES DIRECTLY INTO...
JESUS.
"I DON'T REMEMBER GETTING OUT, PULLING THE RIPCORD, ANY OF IT.
"WHEN I ARRIVED AT EAST GRINSTEAD, THEY SAID I HAD ***STANDARD HURRICANE BURNS.****"*

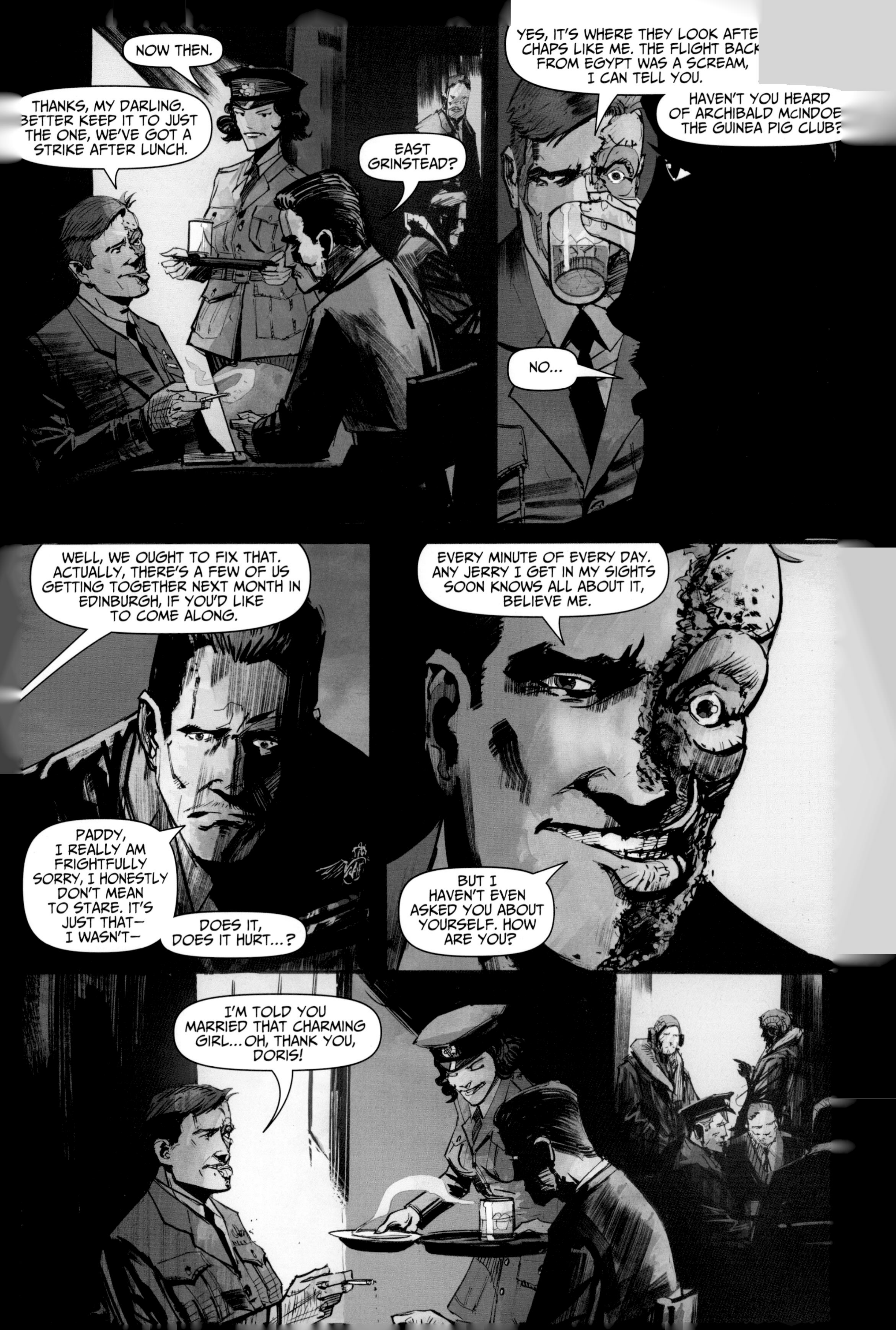
NOW THEN.
THANKS, MY DARLING. BETTER KEEP IT TO JUST THE ONE, WE'VE GOT A STRIKE AFTER LUNCH.
EAST GRINSTEAD?
YES, IT'S WHERE THEY LOOK AFTE CHAPS LIKE ME. THE FLIGHT BACK FROM EGYPT WAS A SCREAM, I CAN TELL YOU.
HAVEN'T YOU HEARD OF ARCHIBALD McINDOE THE GUINEA PIG CLUB?
NO...
WELL, WE OUGHT TO FIX THAT. ACTUALLY, THERE'S A FEW OF US GETTING TOGETHER NEXT MONTH IN EDINBURGH, IF YOU'D LIKE TO COME ALONG.
PADDY, I REALLY AM FRIGHTFULLY SORRY, I HONESTLY DON'T MEAN TO STARE. IT'S JUST THAT— I WASN'T—
DOES IT, DOES IT HURT...?
EVERY MINUTE OF EVERY DAY. ANY JERRY I GET IN MY SIGHTS SOON KNOWS ALL ABOUT IT, BELIEVE ME.
BUT I HAVEN'T EVEN ASKED YOU ABOUT YOURSELF. HOW ARE YOU?
I'M TOLD YOU MARRIED THAT CHARMING GIRL... OH, THANK YOU, DORIS!

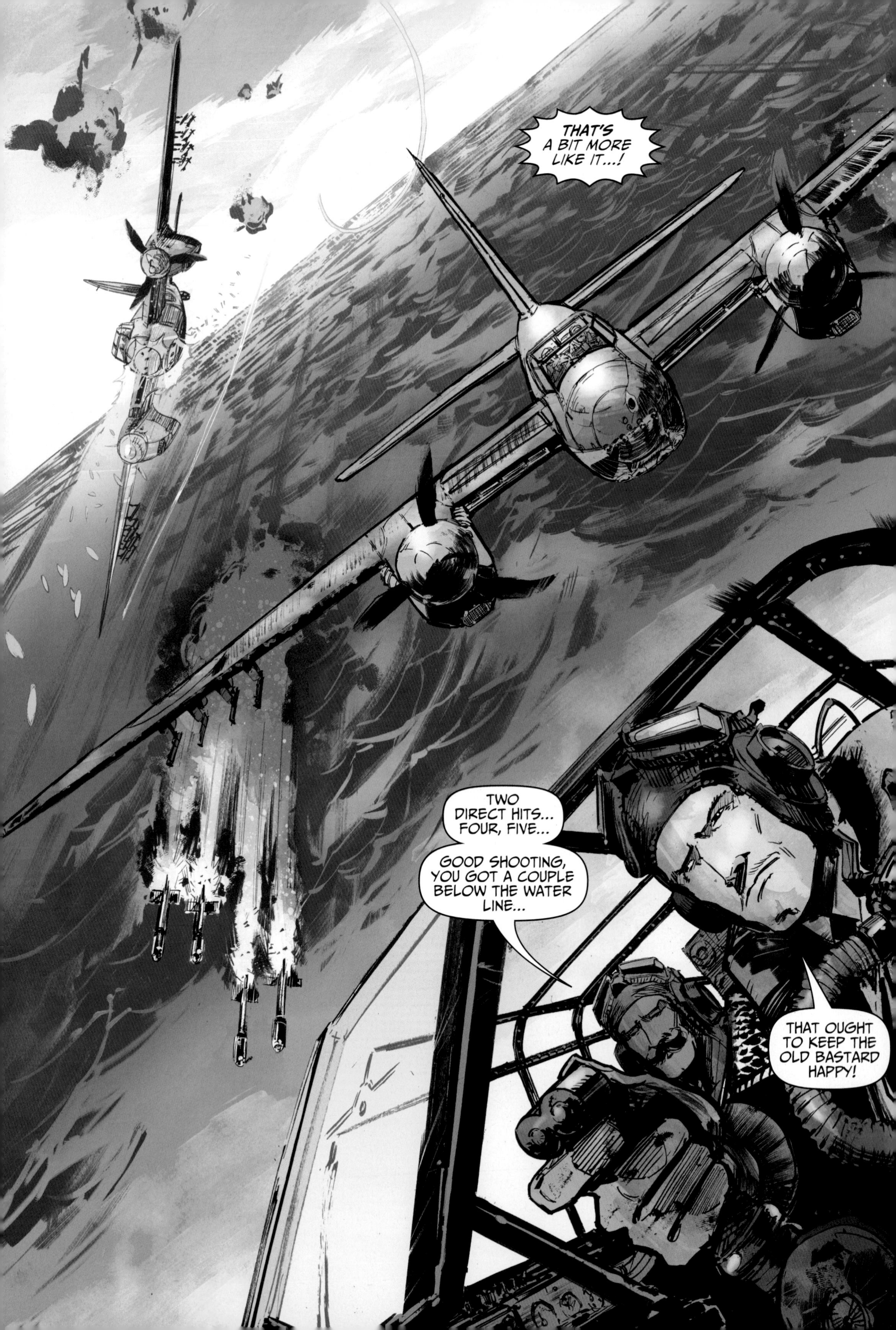
THAT'S A BIT MORE LIKE IT...!
TWO DIRECT HITS... FOUR, FIVE...
GOOD SHOOTING, YOU GOT A COUPLE BELOW THE WATER LINE...
THAT OUGHT TO KEEP THE OLD BASTARD HAPPY!

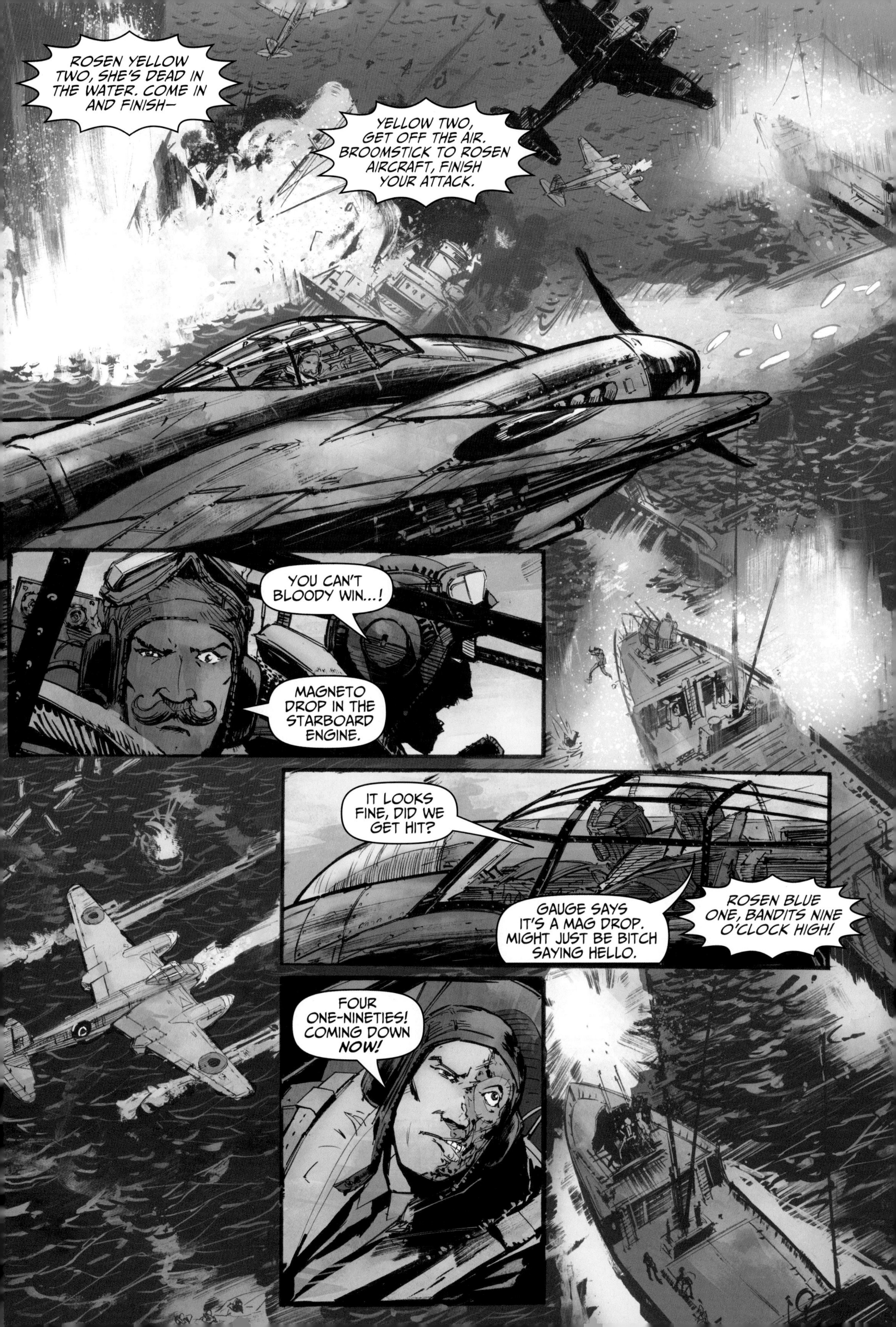
ROSEN YELLOW TWO, SHE'S DEAD IN THE WATER. COME IN AND FINISH–
YELLOW TWO, GET OFF THE AIR. BROOMSTICK TO ROSEN AIRCRAFT, FINISH YOUR ATTACK.
YOU CAN'T BLOODY WIN...!
MAGNETO DROP IN THE STARBOARD ENGINE.
IT LOOKS FINE, DID WE GET HIT?
GAUGE SAYS IT'S A MAG DROP. MIGHT JUST BE BITCH SAYING HELLO.
ROSEN BLUE ONE, BANDITS NINE O'CLOCK HIGH!
FOUR ONE-NINETIES! COMING DOWN NOW!

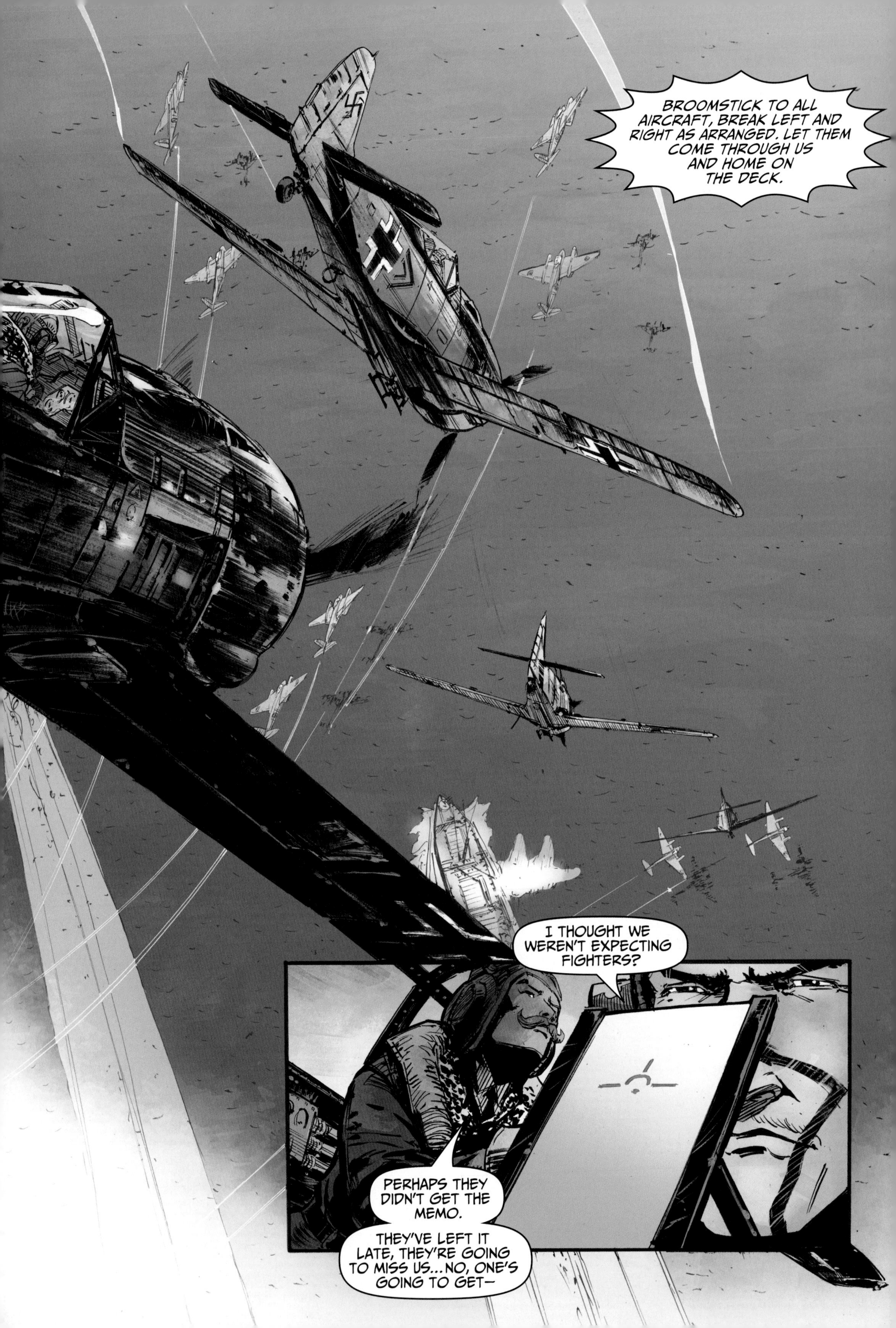

BROOMSTICK TO ALL AIRCRAFT, BREAK LEFT AND RIGHT AS ARRANGED. LET THEM COME THROUGH US AND HOME ON THE DECK.
I THOUGHT WE WEREN'T EXPECTING FIGHTERS?
PERHAPS THEY DIDN'T GET THE MEMO.
THEY'VE LEFT IT LATE, THEY'RE GOING TO MISS US...NO, ONE'S GOING TO GET—

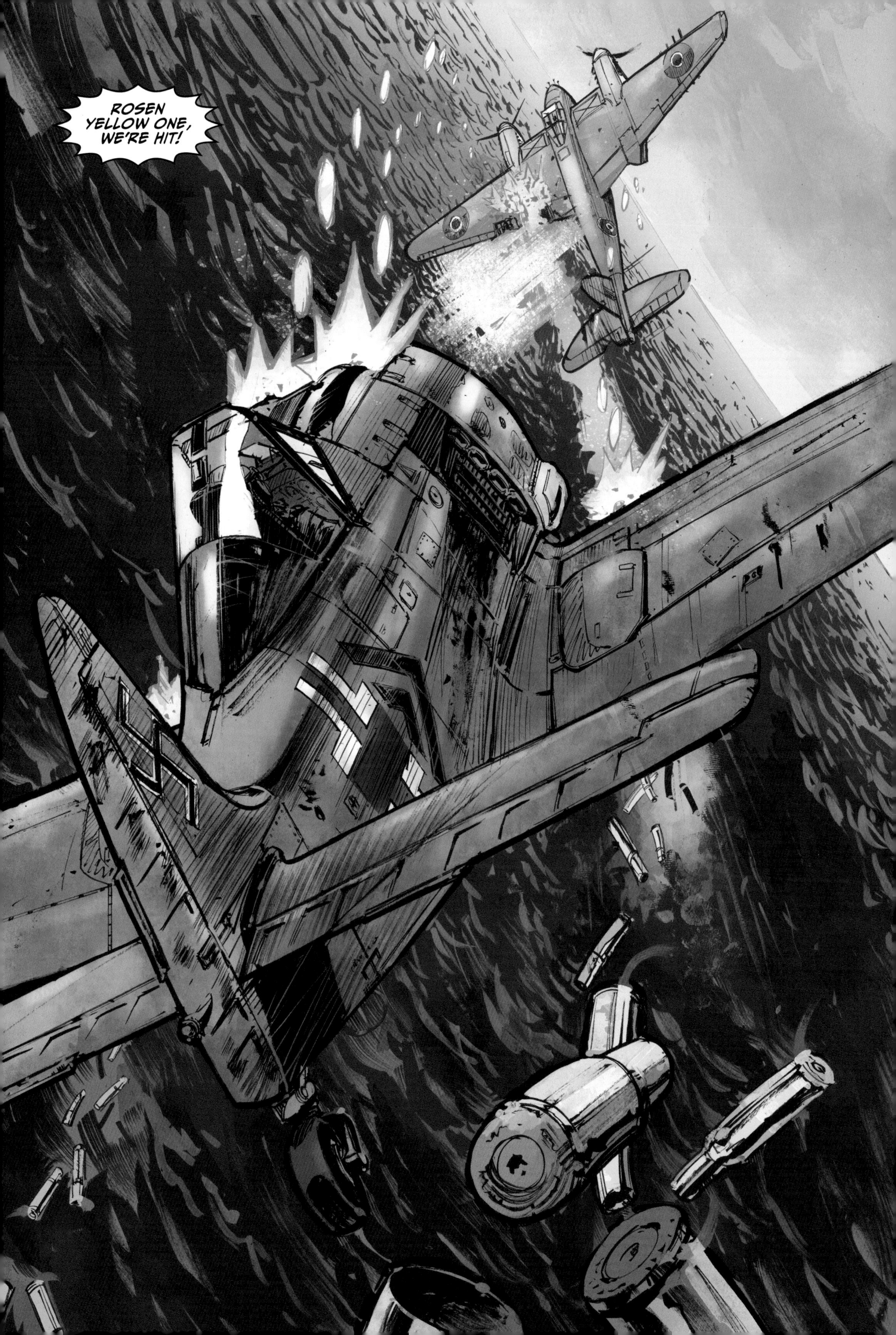
ROSEN YELLOW ONE, WE'RE HIT!

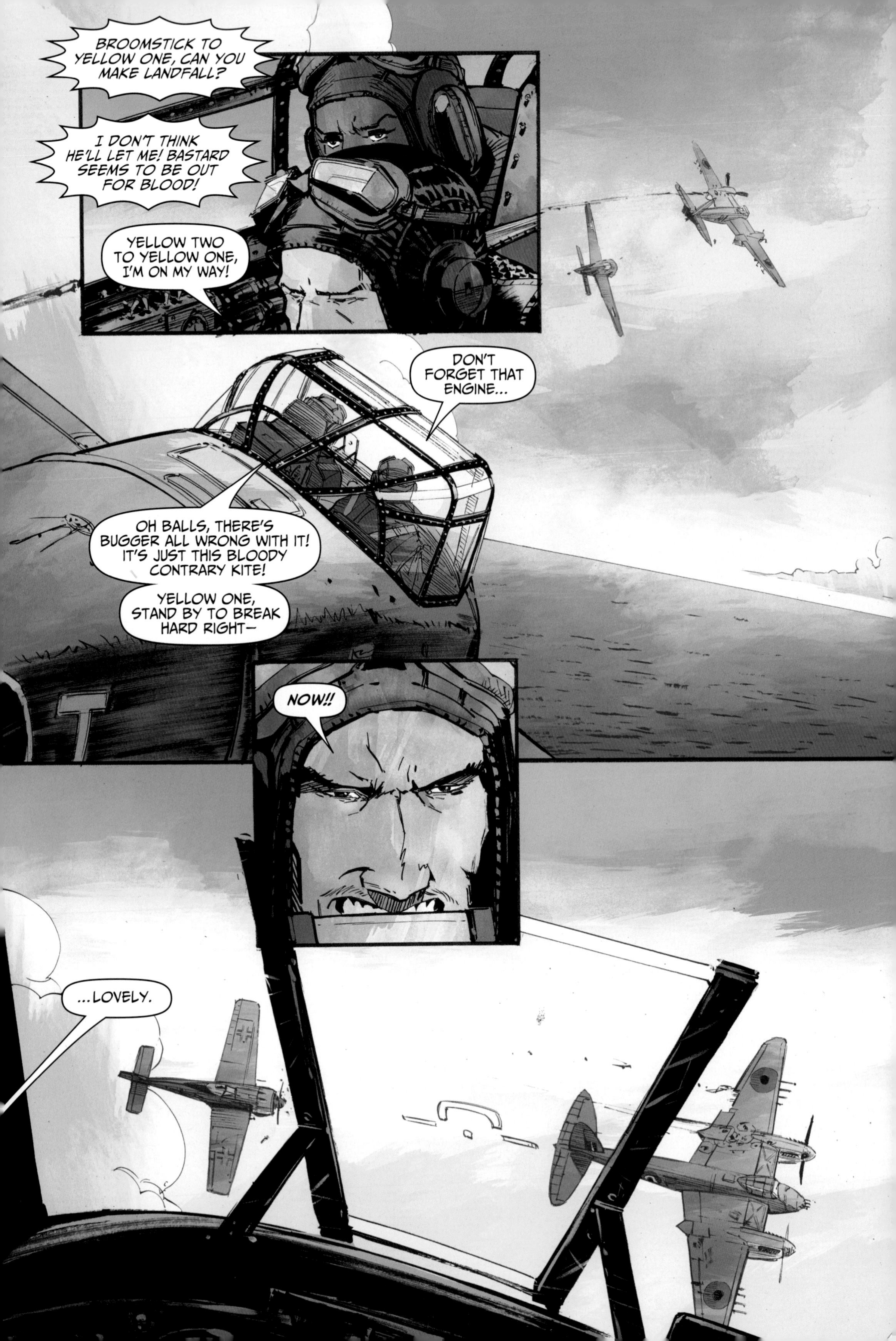
BROOMSTICK TO YELLOW ONE, CAN YOU MAKE LANDFALL?
I DON'T THINK HE'LL LET ME! BASTARD SEEMS TO BE OUT FOR BLOOD!
YELLOW TWO TO YELLOW ONE, I'M ON MY WAY!
DON'T FORGET THAT ENGINE...
OH BALLS, THERE'S BUGGER ALL WRONG WITH IT! IT'S JUST THIS BLOODY CONTRARY KITE!
YELLOW ONE, STAND BY TO BREAK HARD RIGHT–
NOW!!
...LOVELY.

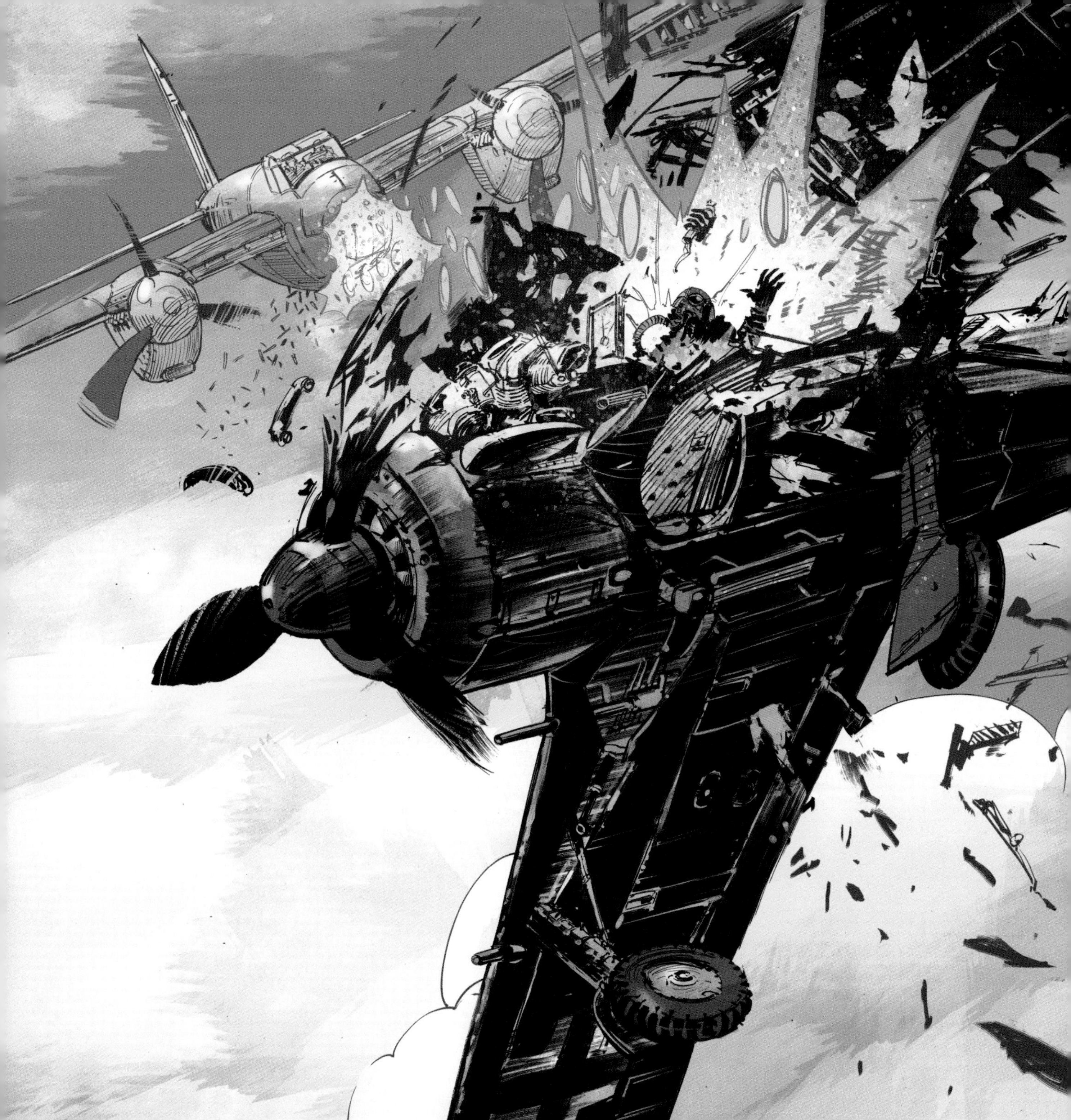

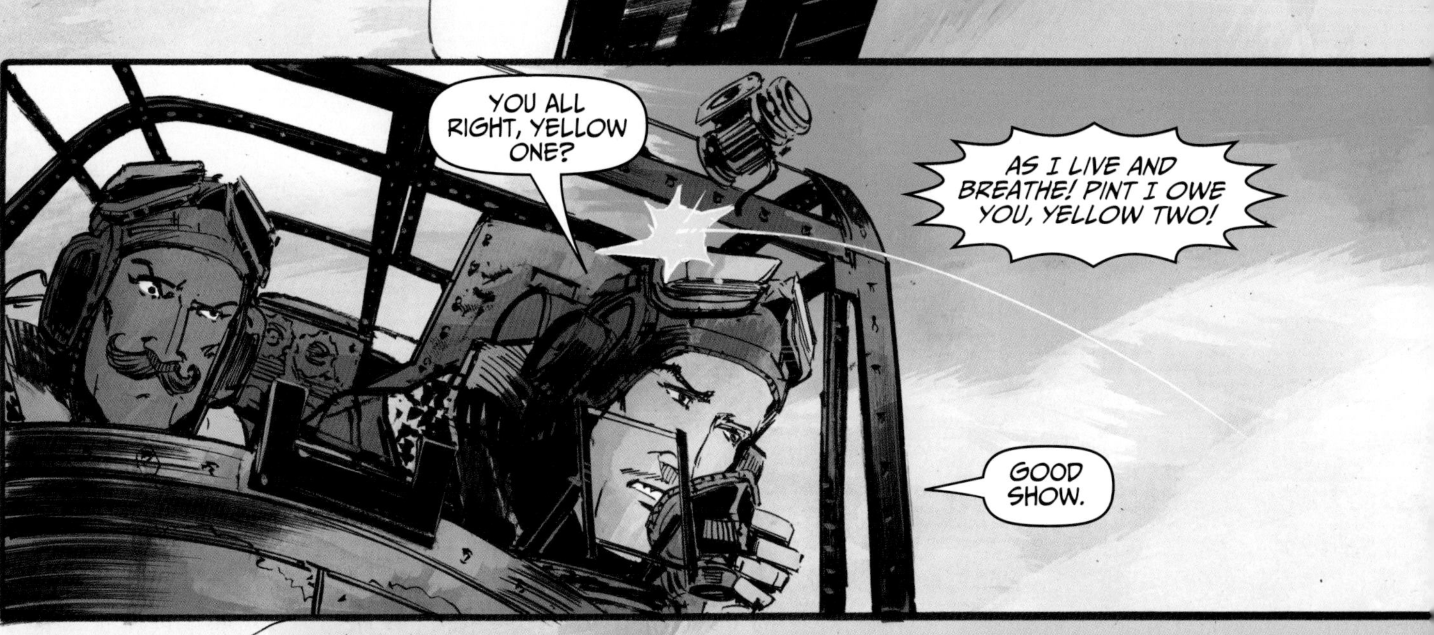
YOU ALL RIGHT, YELLOW ONE?
AS I LIVE AND BREATHE! PINT I OWE YOU, YELLOW TWO!
GOOD SHOW.

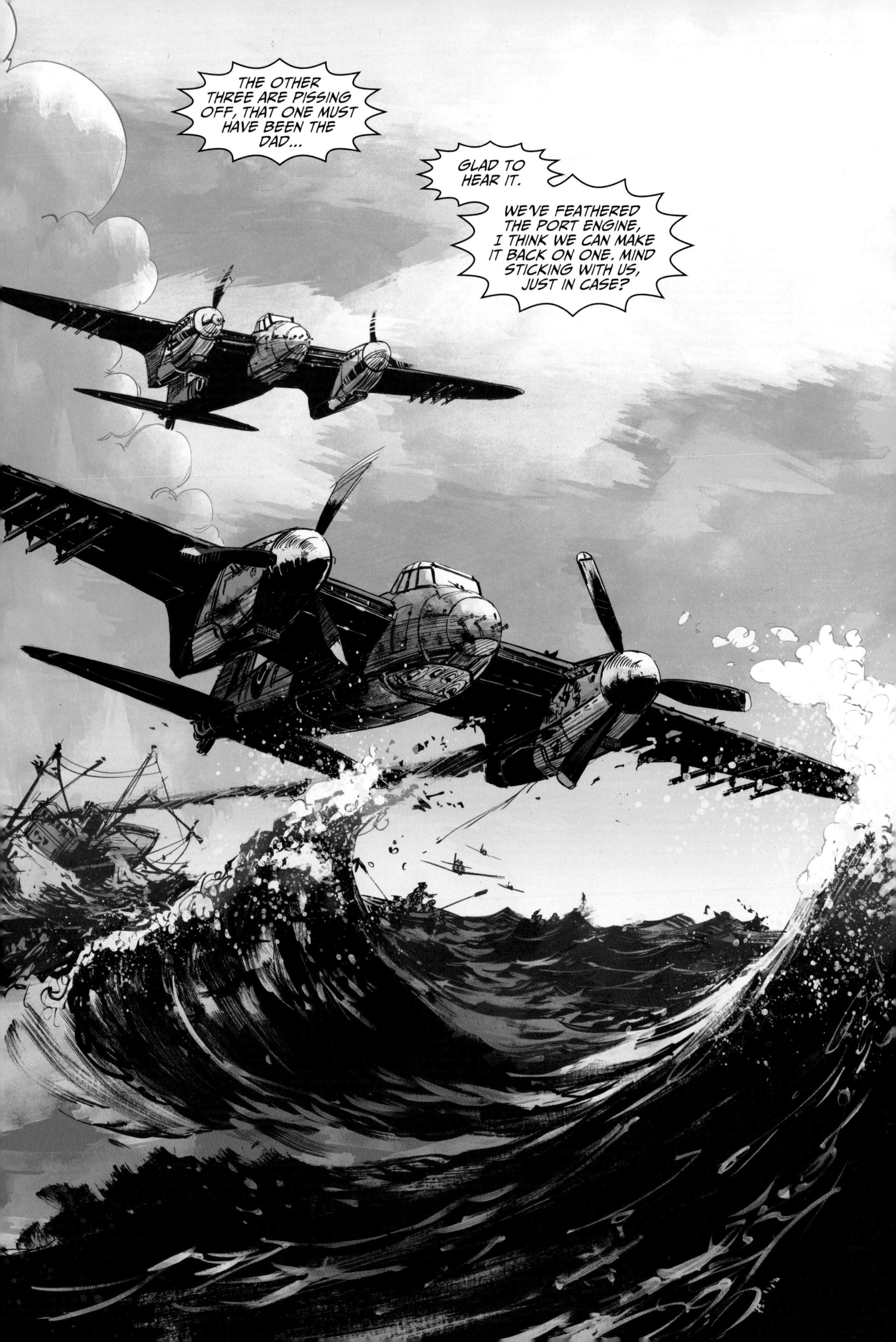
THE OTHER THREE ARE PISSING OFF, THAT ONE MUST HAVE BEEN THE DAD...
GLAD TO HEAR IT.
WE'VE FEATHERED THE PORT ENGINE, I THINK WE CAN MAKE IT BACK ON ONE. MIND STICKING WITH US, JUST IN CASE?

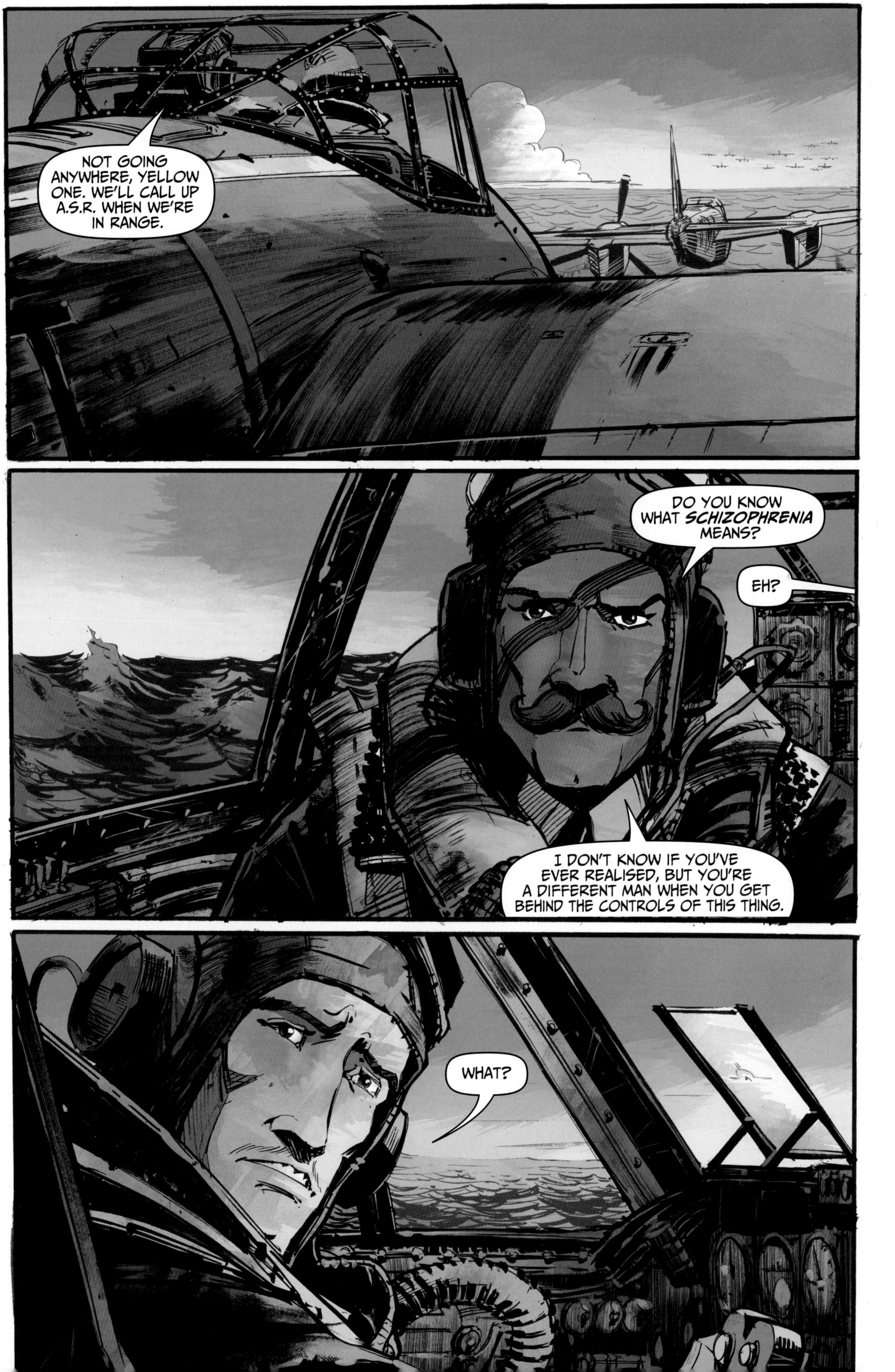
NOT GOING ANYWHERE, YELLOW ONE. WE'LL CALL UP A.S.R. WHEN WE'RE IN RANGE.
DO YOU KNOW WHAT *SCHIZOPHRENIA* MEANS?
EH?
I DON'T KNOW IF YOU'VE EVER REALISED, BUT YOU'RE A DIFFERENT MAN WHEN YOU GET BEHIND THE CONTROLS OF THIS THING.
WHAT?

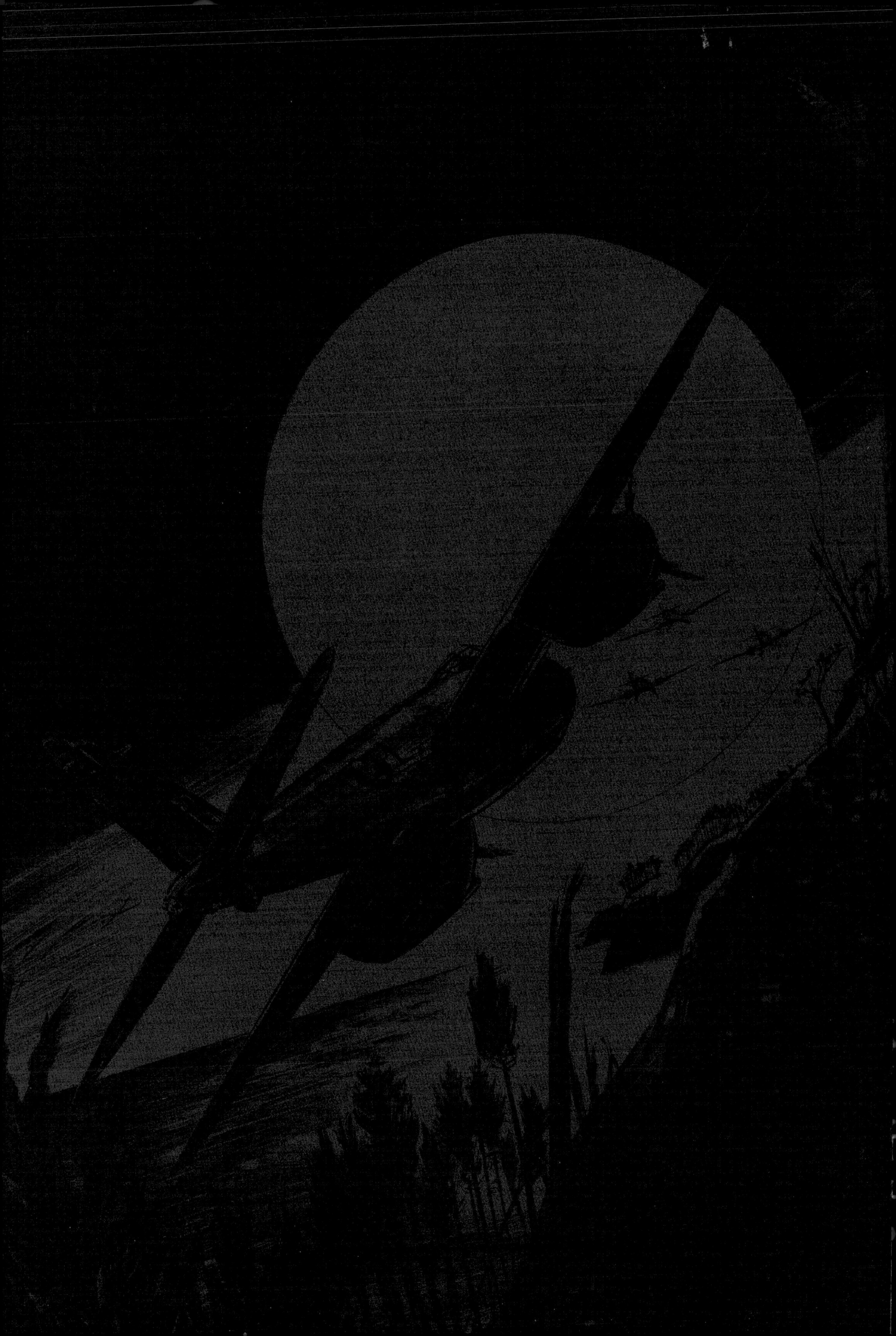

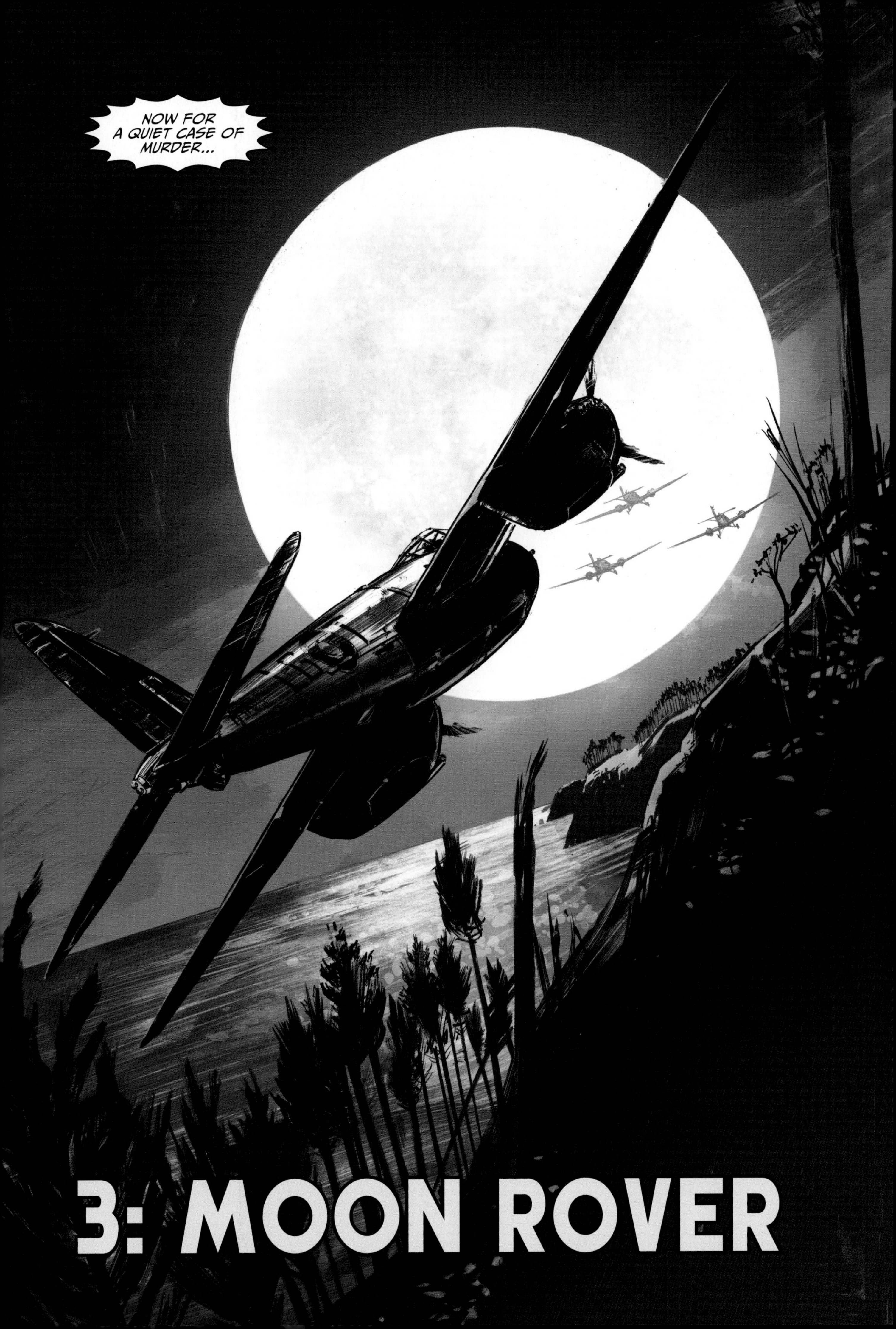
NOW FOR A QUIET CASE OF MURDER...
3: MOON ROVER

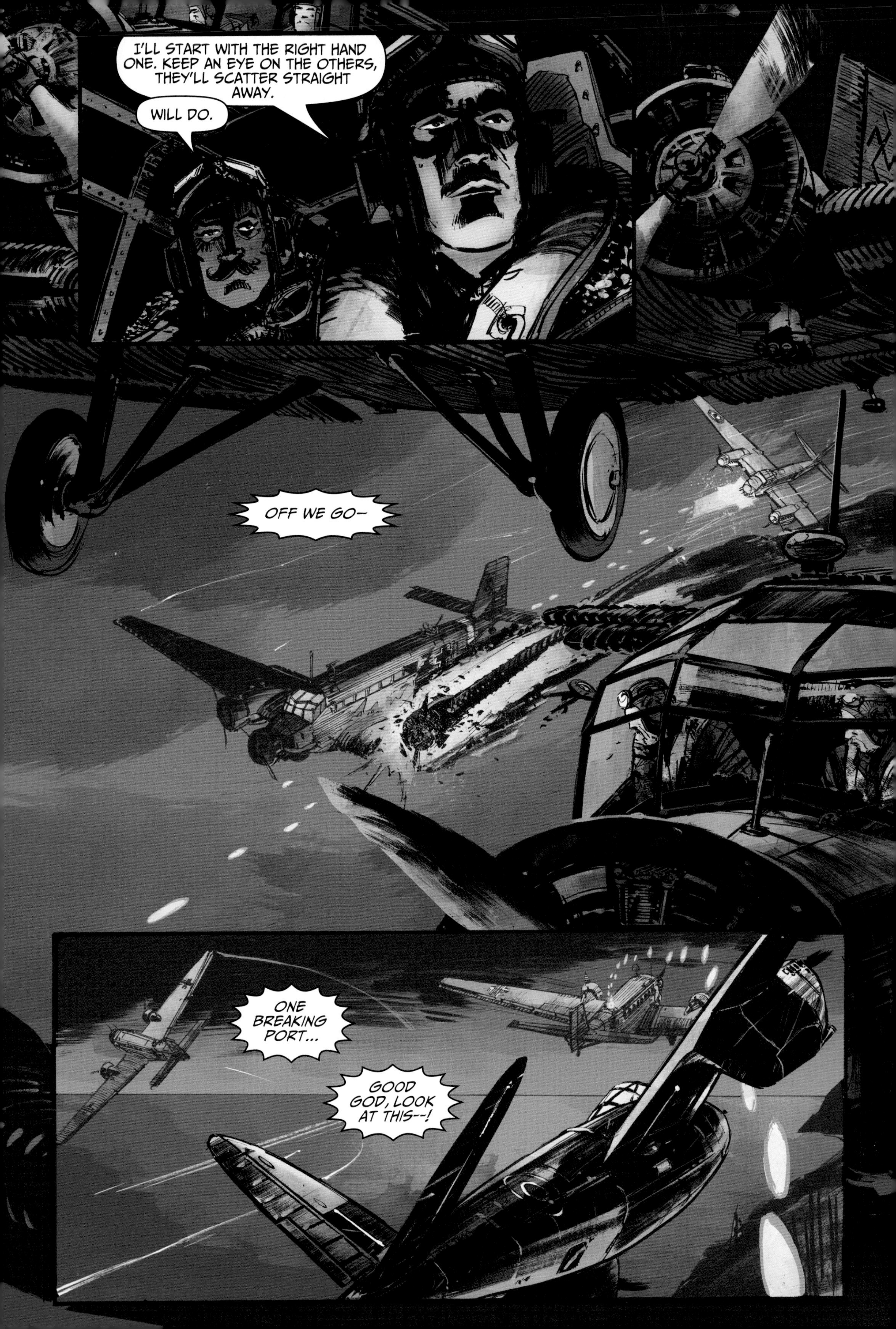
I'LL START WITH THE RIGHT HAND ONE. KEEP AN EYE ON THE OTHERS, THEY'LL SCATTER STRAIGHT AWAY.
WILL DO.
OFF WE GO–
ONE BREAKING PORT...
GOOD GOD, LOOK AT THIS--!

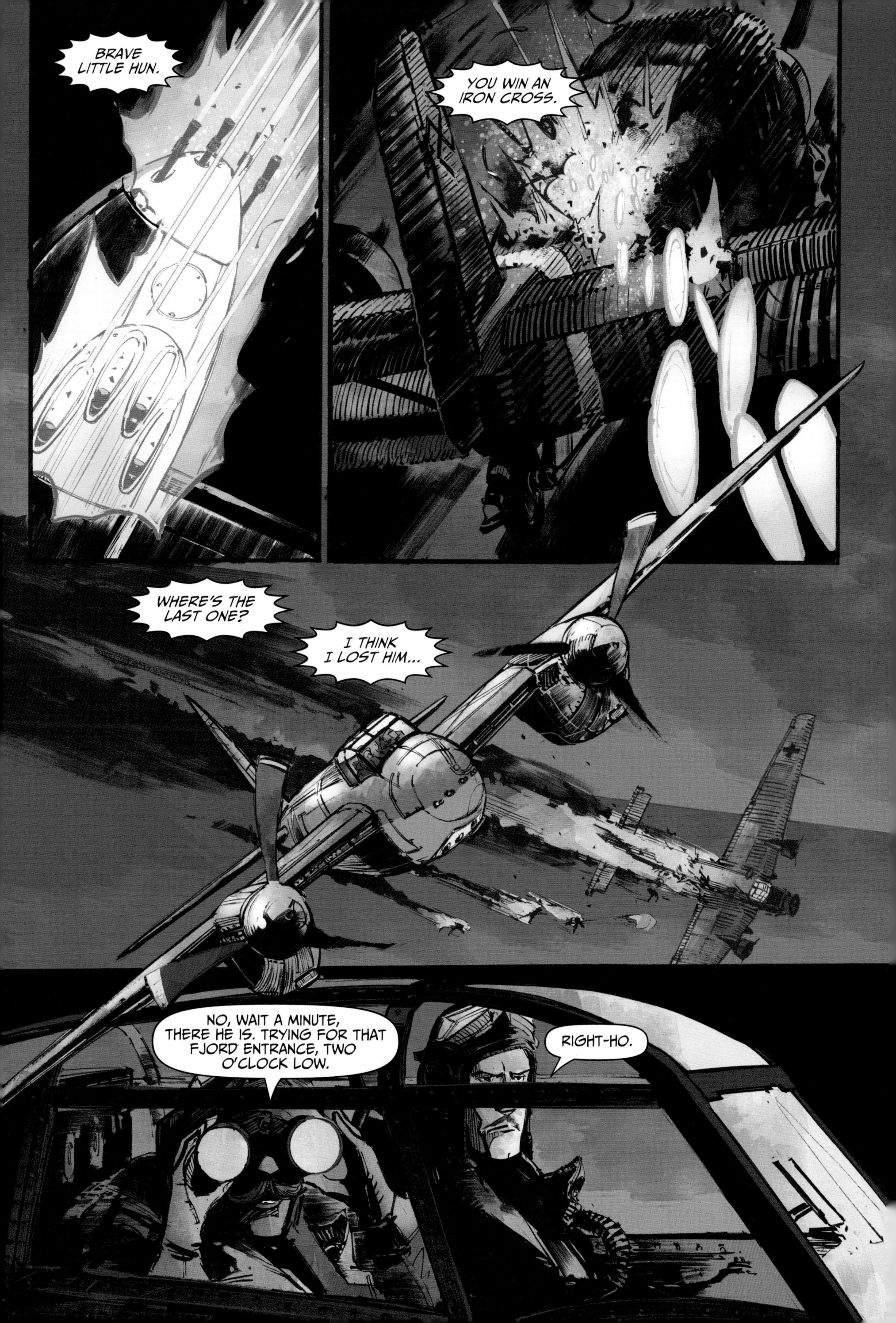
BRAVE LITTLE HUN.
YOU WIN AN IRON CROSS.
WHERE'S THE LAST ONE?
I THINK I LOST HIM...
NO, WAIT A MINUTE, THERE HE IS. TRYING FOR THAT FJORD ENTRANCE, TWO O'CLOCK LOW.
RIGHT-HO.

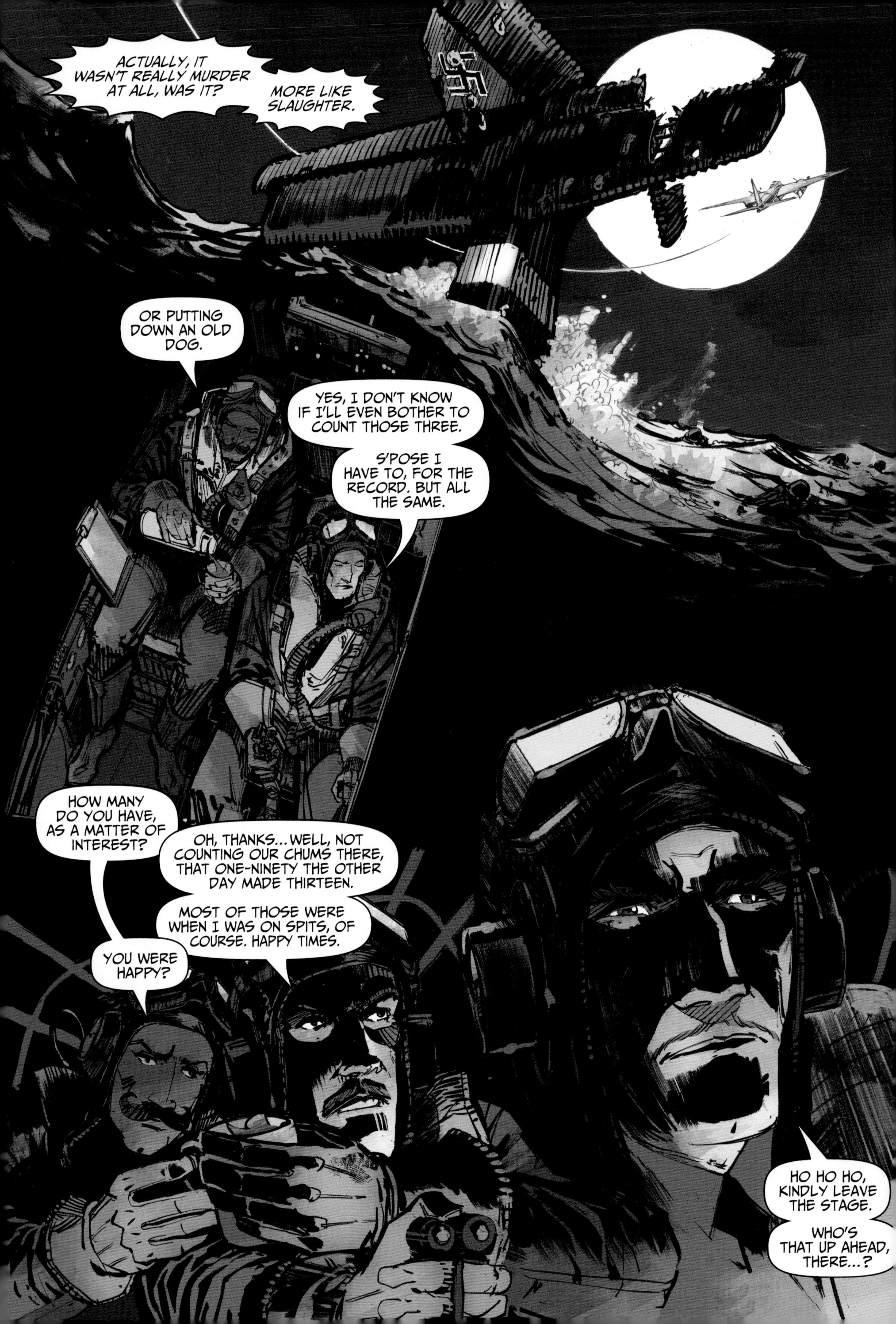
ACTUALLY, IT WASN'T REALLY MURDER AT ALL, WAS IT?
MORE LIKE SLAUGHTER.
OR PUTTING DOWN AN OLD DOG.
YES, I DON'T KNOW IF I'LL EVEN BOTHER TO COUNT THOSE THREE.
S'POSE I HAVE TO, FOR THE RECORD. BUT ALL THE SAME.
HOW MANY DO YOU HAVE, AS A MATTER OF INTEREST?
OH, THANKS... WELL, NOT COUNTING OUR CHUMS THERE, THAT ONE-NINETY THE OTHER DAY MADE THIRTEEN.
MOST OF THOSE WERE WHEN I WAS ON SPITS, OF COURSE. HAPPY TIMES.
YOU WERE HAPPY?
HO HO HO, KINDLY LEAVE THE STAGE.
WHO'S THAT UP AHEAD, THERE...?

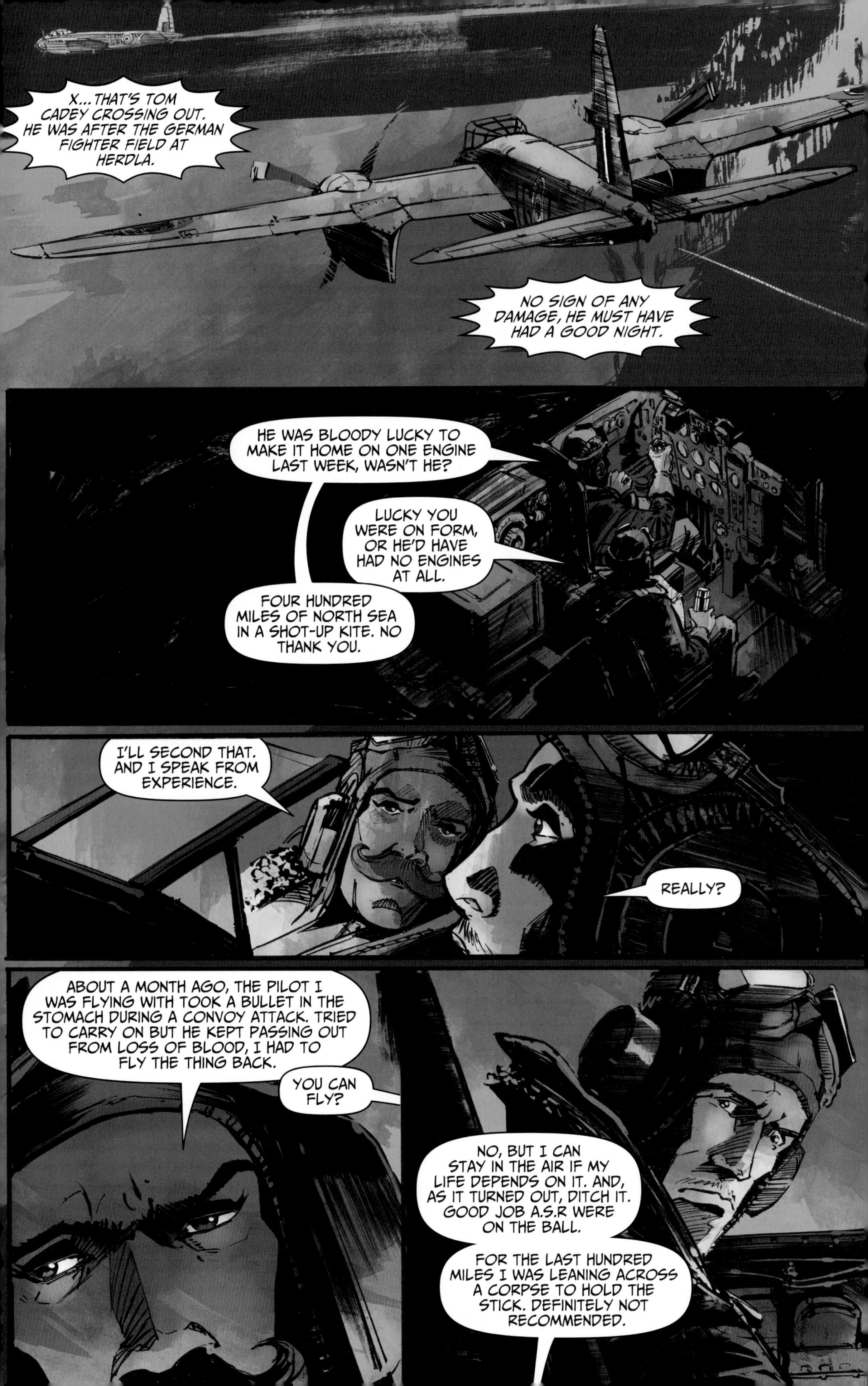
X...THAT'S TOM CADEY CROSSING OUT. HE WAS AFTER THE GERMAN FIGHTER FIELD AT HERDLA.
NO SIGN OF ANY DAMAGE, HE MUST HAVE HAD A GOOD NIGHT.
HE WAS BLOODY LUCKY TO MAKE IT HOME ON ONE ENGINE LAST WEEK, WASN'T HE?
LUCKY YOU WERE ON FORM, OR HE'D HAVE HAD NO ENGINES AT ALL.
FOUR HUNDRED MILES OF NORTH SEA IN A SHOT-UP KITE. NO THANK YOU.
I'LL SECOND THAT. AND I SPEAK FROM EXPERIENCE.
REALLY?
ABOUT A MONTH AGO, THE PILOT I WAS FLYING WITH TOOK A BULLET IN THE STOMACH DURING A CONVOY ATTACK. TRIED TO CARRY ON BUT HE KEPT PASSING OUT FROM LOSS OF BLOOD, I HAD TO FLY THE THING BACK.
YOU CAN FLY?
NO, BUT I CAN STAY IN THE AIR IF MY LIFE DEPENDS ON IT. AND, AS IT TURNED OUT, DITCH IT. GOOD JOB A.S.R WERE ON THE BALL.
FOR THE LAST HUNDRED MILES I WAS LEANING ACROSS A CORPSE TO HOLD THE STICK. DEFINITELY NOT RECOMMENDED.

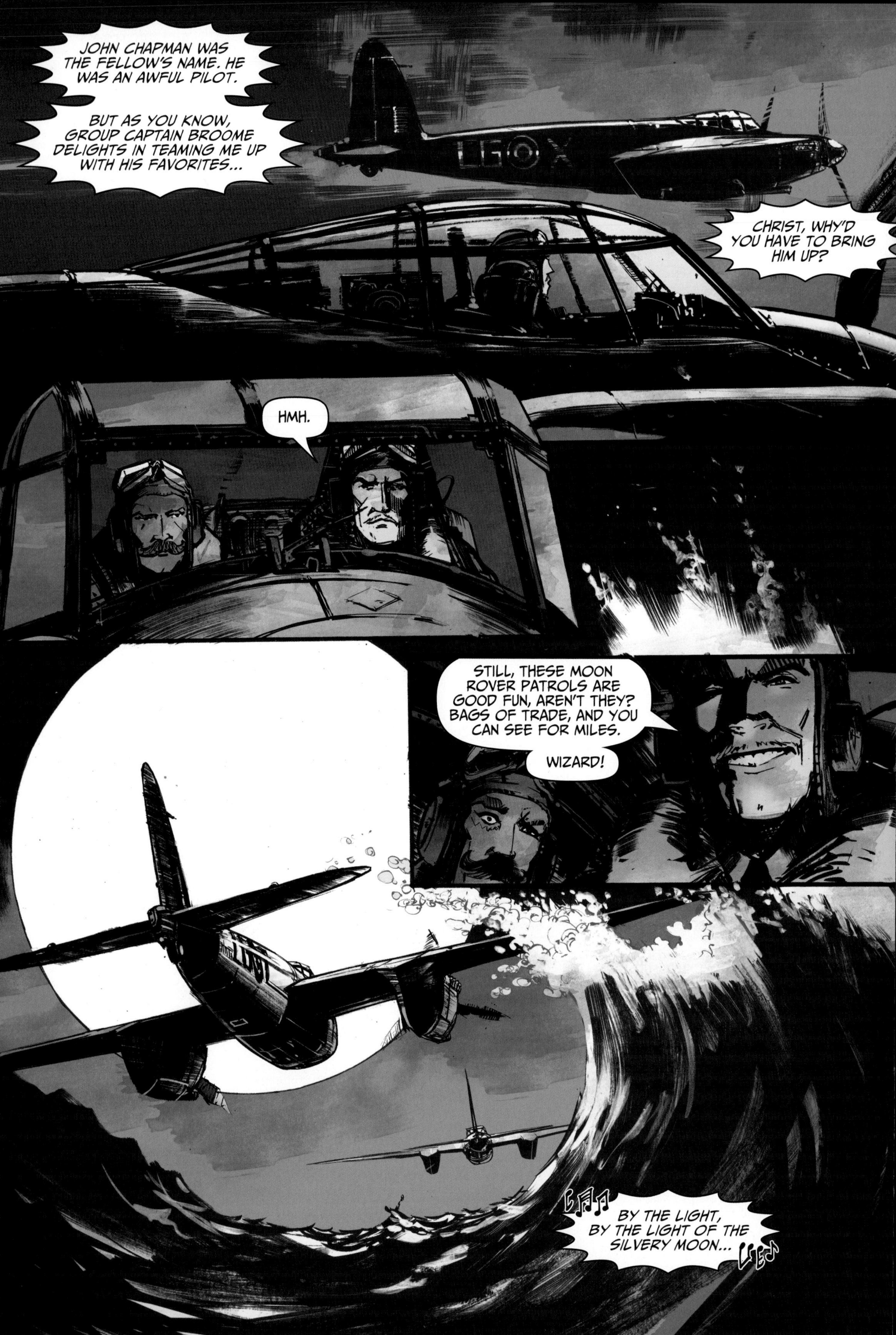
JOHN CHAPMAN WAS THE FELLOW'S NAME. HE WAS AN AWFUL PILOT.
BUT AS YOU KNOW, GROUP CAPTAIN BROOME DELIGHTS IN TEAMING ME UP WITH HIS FAVORITES...
CHRIST, WHY'D YOU HAVE TO BRING HIM UP?
HMH.
STILL, THESE MOON ROVER PATROLS ARE GOOD FUN, AREN'T THEY? BAGS OF TRADE, AND YOU CAN SEE FOR MILES.
WIZARD!
BY THE LIGHT, BY THE LIGHT OF THE SILVERY MOON...

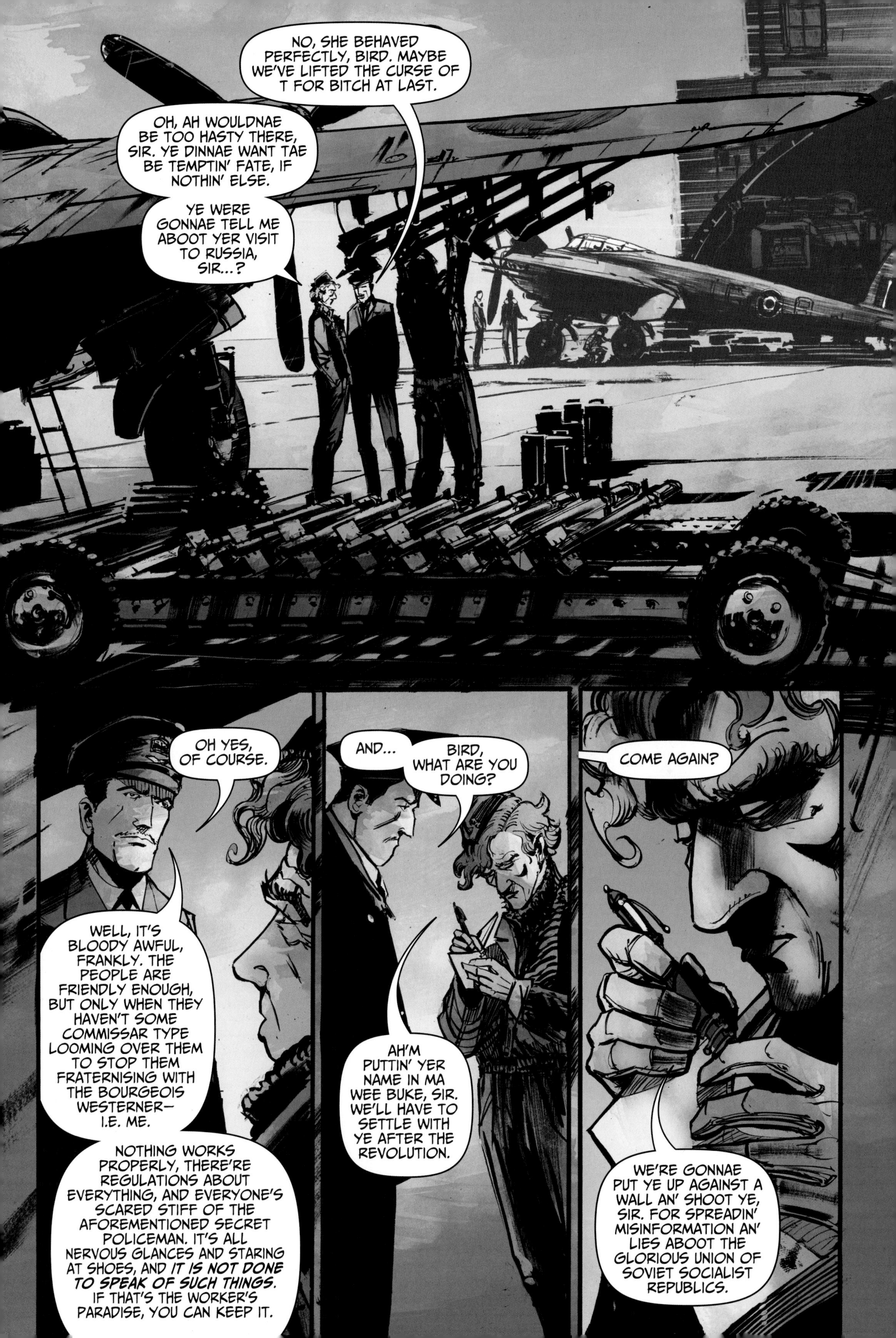
NO, SHE BEHAVED PERFECTLY, BIRD. MAYBE WE'VE LIFTED THE CURSE OF T FOR BITCH AT LAST.
OH, AH WOULDNAE BE TOO HASTY THERE, SIR. YE DINNAE WANT TAE BE TEMPTIN' FATE, IF NOTHIN' ELSE.
YE WERE GONNAE TELL ME ABOOT YER VISIT TO RUSSIA, SIR...?
OH YES, OF COURSE.
WELL, IT'S BLOODY AWFUL, FRANKLY. THE PEOPLE ARE FRIENDLY ENOUGH, BUT ONLY WHEN THEY HAVEN'T SOME COMMISSAR TYPE LOOMING OVER THEM TO STOP THEM FRATERNISING WITH THE BOURGEOIS WESTERNER— I.E. ME.
NOTHING WORKS PROPERLY, THERE'RE REGULATIONS ABOUT EVERYTHING, AND EVERYONE'S SCARED STIFF OF THE AFOREMENTIONED SECRET POLICEMAN. IT'S ALL NERVOUS GLANCES AND STARING AT SHOES, AND *IT IS NOT DONE TO SPEAK OF SUCH THINGS*. IF THAT'S THE WORKER'S PARADISE, YOU CAN KEEP IT.
AND...
BIRD, WHAT ARE YOU DOING?
AH'M PUTTIN' YER NAME IN MA WEE BUKE, SIR. WE'LL HAVE TO SETTLE WITH YE AFTER THE REVOLUTION.
COME AGAIN?
WE'RE GONNAE PUT YE UP AGAINST A WALL AN' SHOOT YE, SIR. FOR SPREADIN' MISINFORMATION AN' LIES ABOOT THE GLORIOUS UNION OF SOVIET SOCIALIST REPUBLICS.

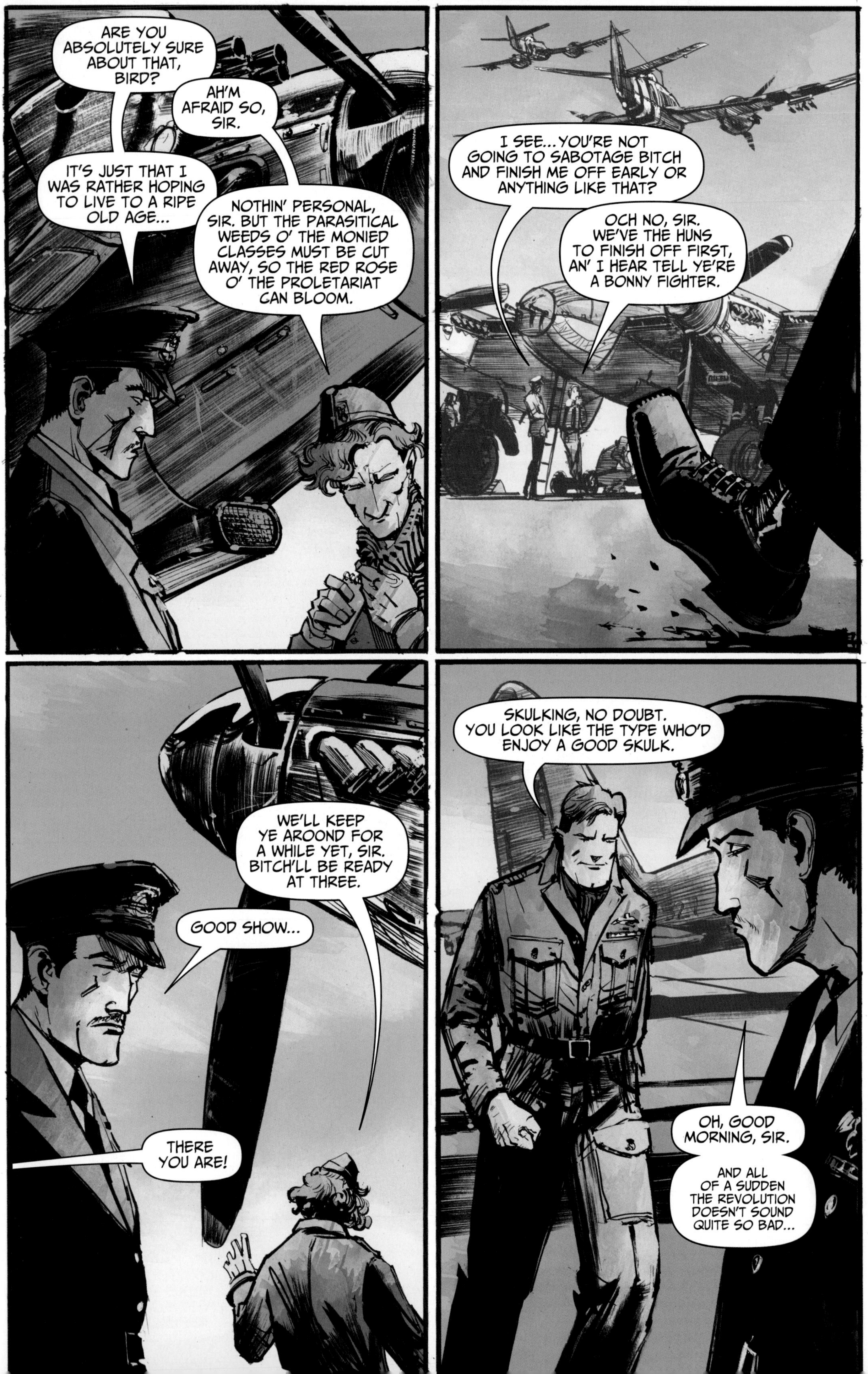
ARE YOU ABSOLUTELY SURE ABOUT THAT, BIRD?
AH'M AFRAID SO, SIR.
IT'S JUST THAT I WAS RATHER HOPING TO LIVE TO A RIPE OLD AGE...
NOTHIN' PERSONAL, SIR. BUT THE PARASITICAL WEEDS O' THE MONIED CLASSES MUST BE CUT AWAY, SO THE RED ROSE O' THE PROLETARIAT CAN BLOOM.
I SEE... YOU'RE NOT GOING TO SABOTAGE BITCH AND FINISH ME OFF EARLY OR ANYTHING LIKE THAT?
OCH NO, SIR. WE'VE THE HUNS TO FINISH OFF FIRST, AN' I HEAR TELL YE'RE A BONNY FIGHTER.
WE'LL KEEP YE AROOND FOR A WHILE YET, SIR. BITCH'LL BE READY AT THREE.
GOOD SHOW...
THERE YOU ARE!
SKULKING, NO DOUBT. YOU LOOK LIKE THE TYPE WHO'D ENJOY A GOOD SKULK.
OH, GOOD MORNING, SIR.
AND ALL OF A SUDDEN THE REVOLUTION DOESN'T SOUND QUITE SO BAD...

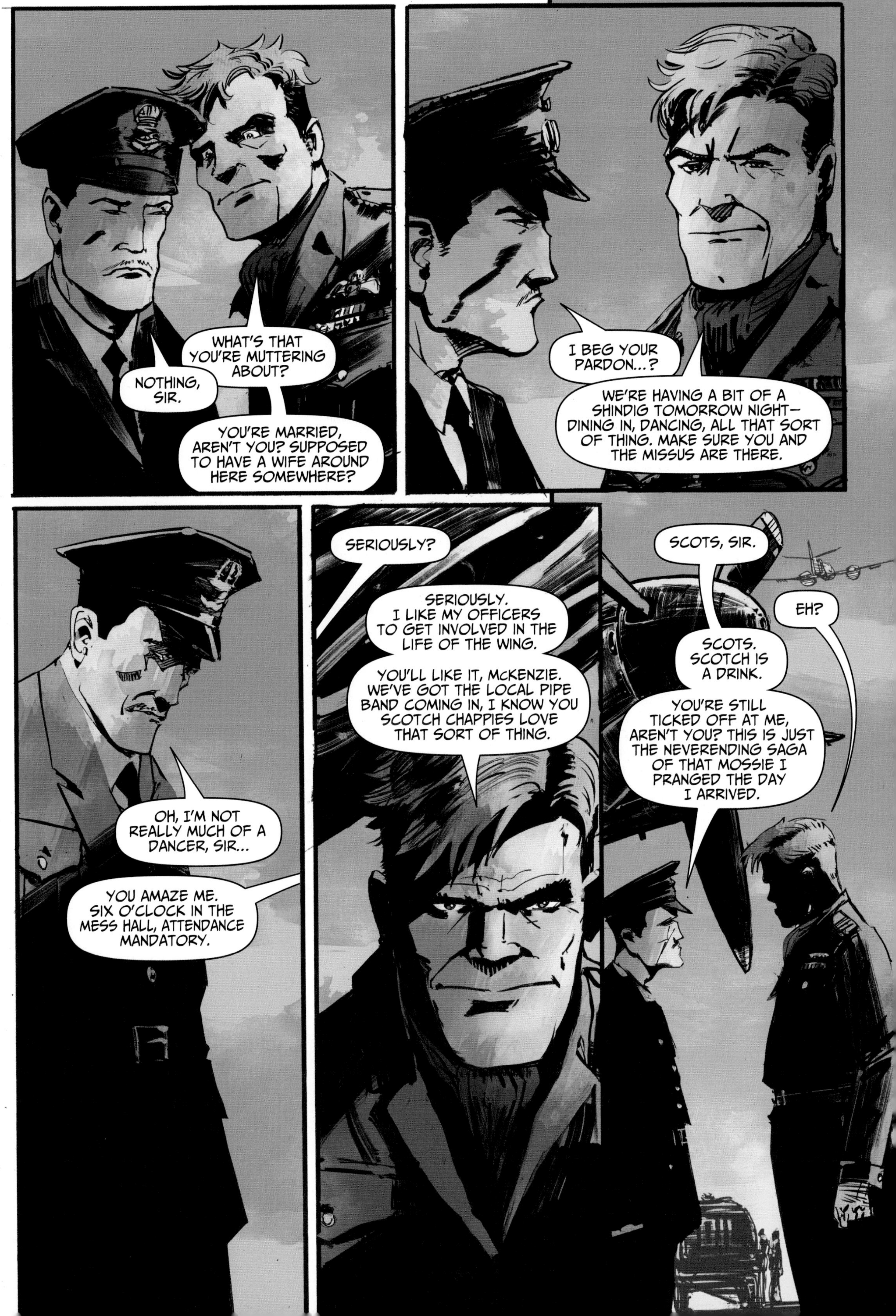
WHAT'S THAT YOU'RE MUTTERING ABOUT?
NOTHING, SIR.
YOU'RE MARRIED, AREN'T YOU? SUPPOSED TO HAVE A WIFE AROUND HERE SOMEWHERE?
I BEG YOUR PARDON...?
WE'RE HAVING A BIT OF A SHINDIG TOMORROW NIGHT– DINING IN, DANCING, ALL THAT SORT OF THING. MAKE SURE YOU AND THE MISSUS ARE THERE.
OH, I'M NOT REALLY MUCH OF A DANCER, SIR...
YOU AMAZE ME. SIX O'CLOCK IN THE MESS HALL, ATTENDANCE MANDATORY.
SERIOUSLY?
SERIOUSLY. I LIKE MY OFFICERS TO GET INVOLVED IN THE LIFE OF THE WING.
YOU'LL LIKE IT, McKENZIE. WE'VE GOT THE LOCAL PIPE BAND COMING IN, I KNOW YOU SCOTCH CHAPPIES LOVE THAT SORT OF THING.
SCOTS, SIR.
EH?
SCOTS. SCOTCH IS A DRINK.
YOU'RE STILL TICKED OFF AT ME, AREN'T YOU? THIS IS JUST THE NEVERENDING SAGA OF THAT MOSSIE I PRANGED THE DAY I ARRIVED.

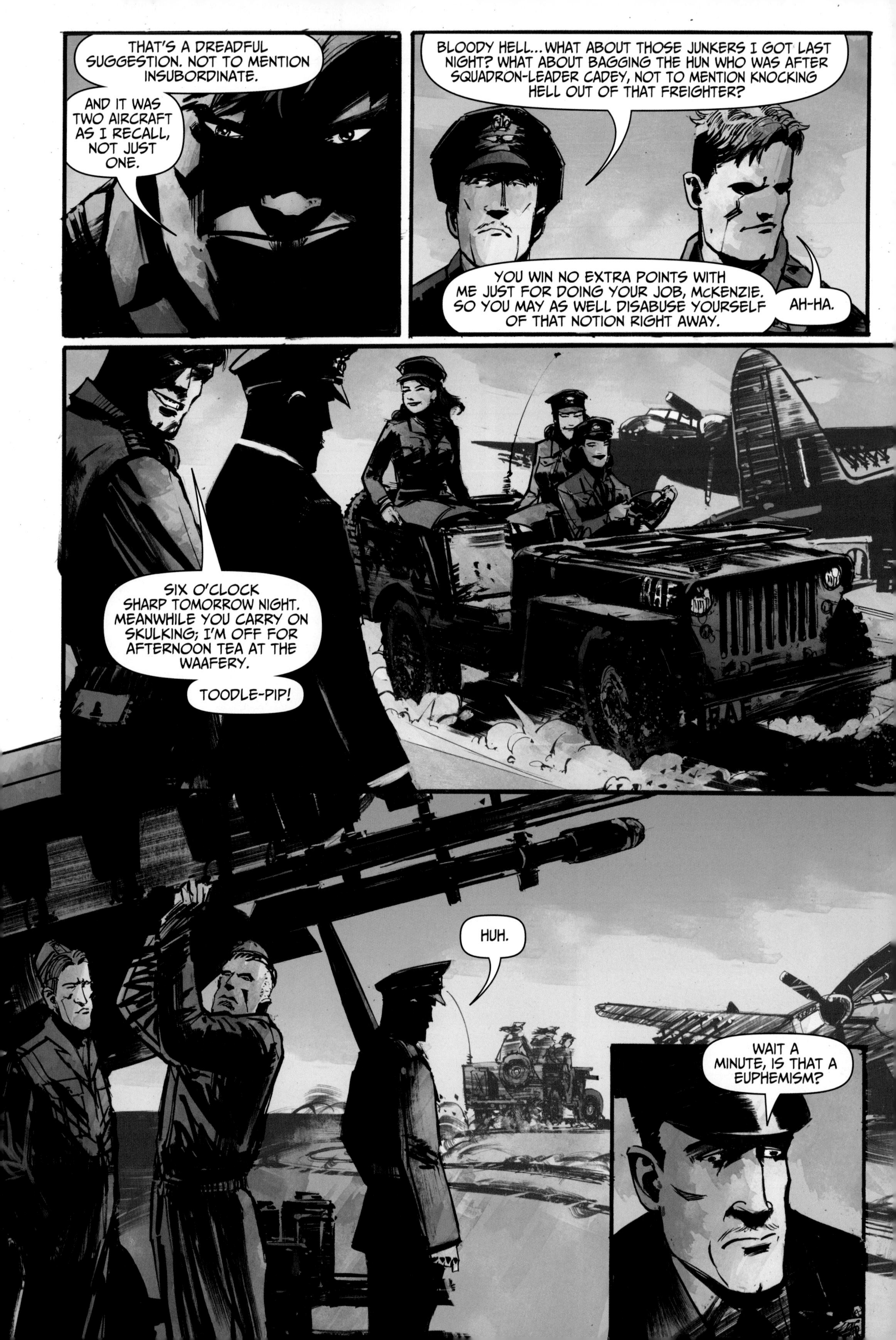
THAT'S A DREADFUL SUGGESTION. NOT TO MENTION INSUBORDINATE.
AND IT WAS TWO AIRCRAFT AS I RECALL, NOT JUST ONE.
BLOODY HELL...WHAT ABOUT THOSE JUNKERS I GOT LAST NIGHT? WHAT ABOUT BAGGING THE HUN WHO WAS AFTER SQUADRON-LEADER CADEY, NOT TO MENTION KNOCKING HELL OUT OF THAT FREIGHTER?
YOU WIN NO EXTRA POINTS WITH ME JUST FOR DOING YOUR JOB, McKENZIE. SO YOU MAY AS WELL DISABUSE YOURSELF OF THAT NOTION RIGHT AWAY.
AH-HA.
SIX O'CLOCK SHARP TOMORROW NIGHT. MEANWHILE YOU CARRY ON SKULKING; I'M OFF FOR AFTERNOON TEA AT THE WAAFERY.
TOODLE-PIP!
RAF
HUH.
WAIT A MINUTE, IS THAT A EUPHEMISM?

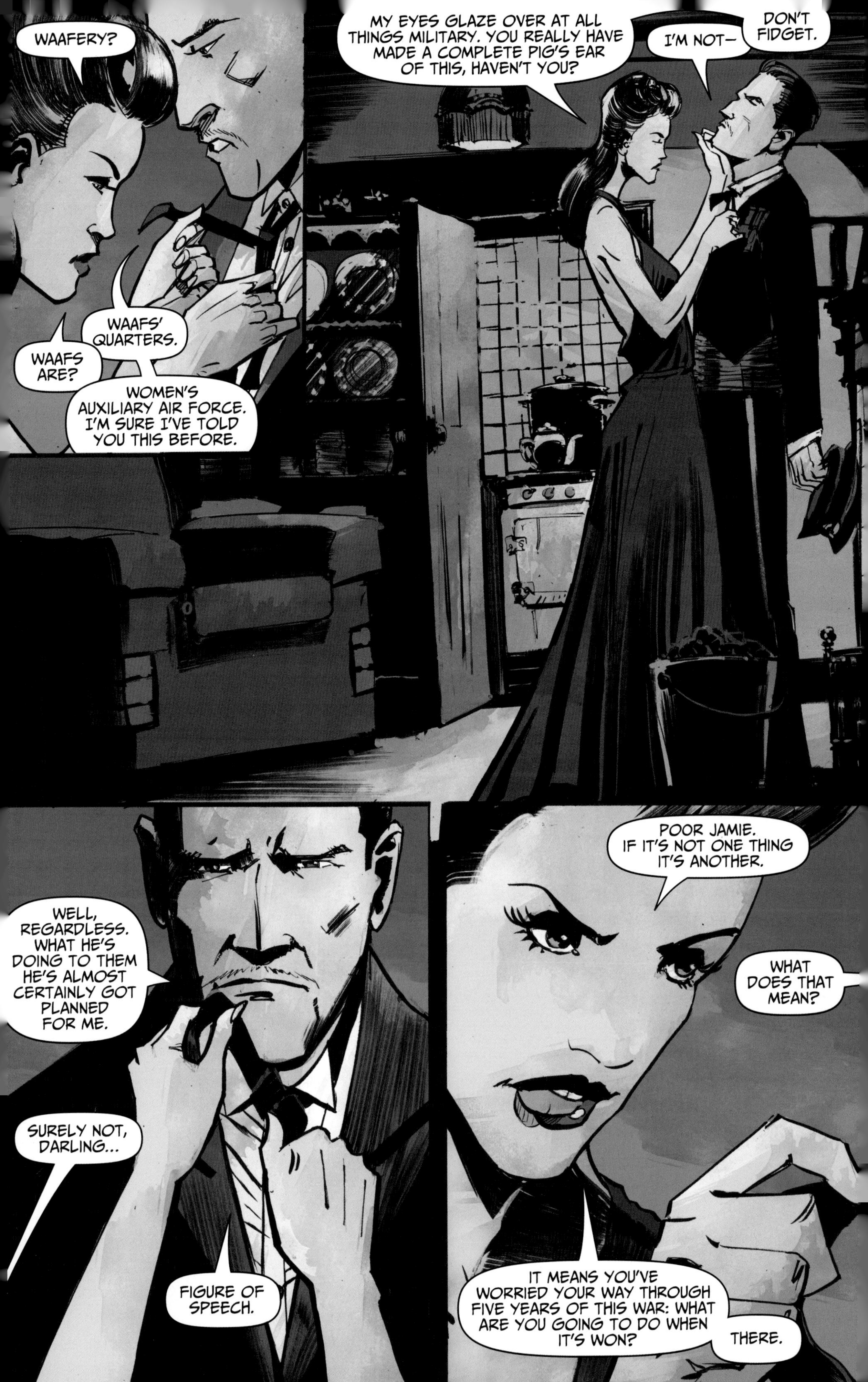
WAAFERY?
WAAFS' QUARTERS.
WAAFS ARE?
WOMEN'S AUXILIARY AIR FORCE. I'M SURE I'VE TOLD YOU THIS BEFORE.
MY EYES GLAZE OVER AT ALL THINGS MILITARY. YOU REALLY HAVE MADE A COMPLETE PIG'S EAR OF THIS, HAVEN'T YOU?
I'M NOT—
DON'T FIDGET.
WELL, REGARDLESS. WHAT HE'S DOING TO THEM HE'S ALMOST CERTAINLY GOT PLANNED FOR ME.
SURELY NOT, DARLING...
FIGURE OF SPEECH.
POOR JAMIE. IF IT'S NOT ONE THING IT'S ANOTHER.
WHAT DOES THAT MEAN?
IT MEANS YOU'VE WORRIED YOUR WAY THROUGH FIVE YEARS OF THIS WAR: WHAT ARE YOU GOING TO DO WHEN IT'S WON?
THERE.

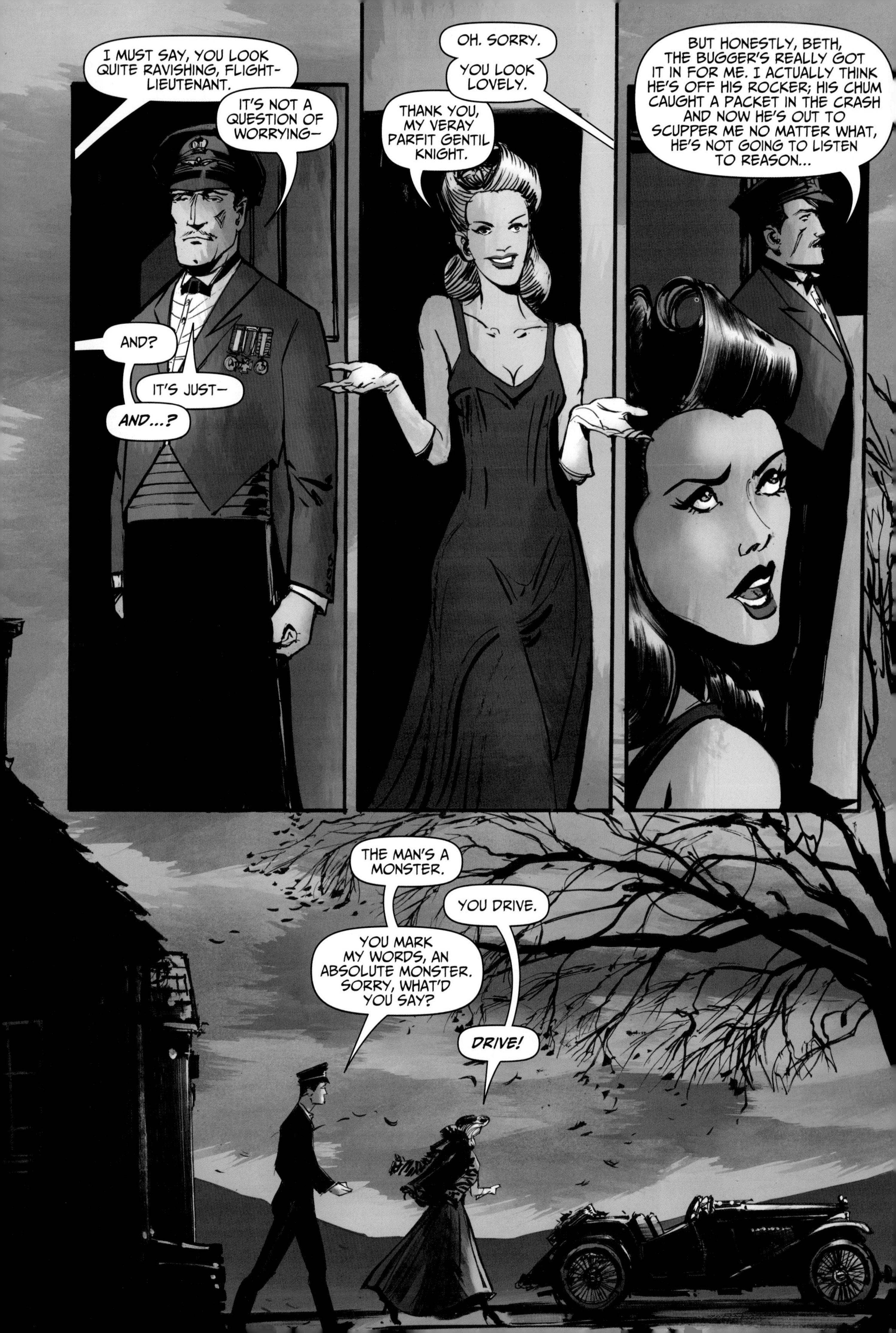
I MUST SAY, YOU LOOK QUITE RAVISHING, FLIGHT-LIEUTENANT.
IT'S NOT A QUESTION OF WORRYING—
AND?
IT'S JUST—
AND...?
OH. SORRY.
YOU LOOK LOVELY.
THANK YOU, MY VERAY PARFIT GENTIL KNIGHT.
BUT HONESTLY, BETH, THE BUGGER'S REALLY GOT IT IN FOR ME. I ACTUALLY THINK HE'S OFF HIS ROCKER; HIS CHUM CAUGHT A PACKET IN THE CRASH AND NOW HE'S OUT TO SCUPPER ME NO MATTER WHAT, HE'S NOT GOING TO LISTEN TO REASON...
THE MAN'S A MONSTER.
YOU DRIVE.
YOU MARK MY WORDS, AN ABSOLUTE MONSTER. SORRY, WHAT'D YOU SAY?
DRIVE!

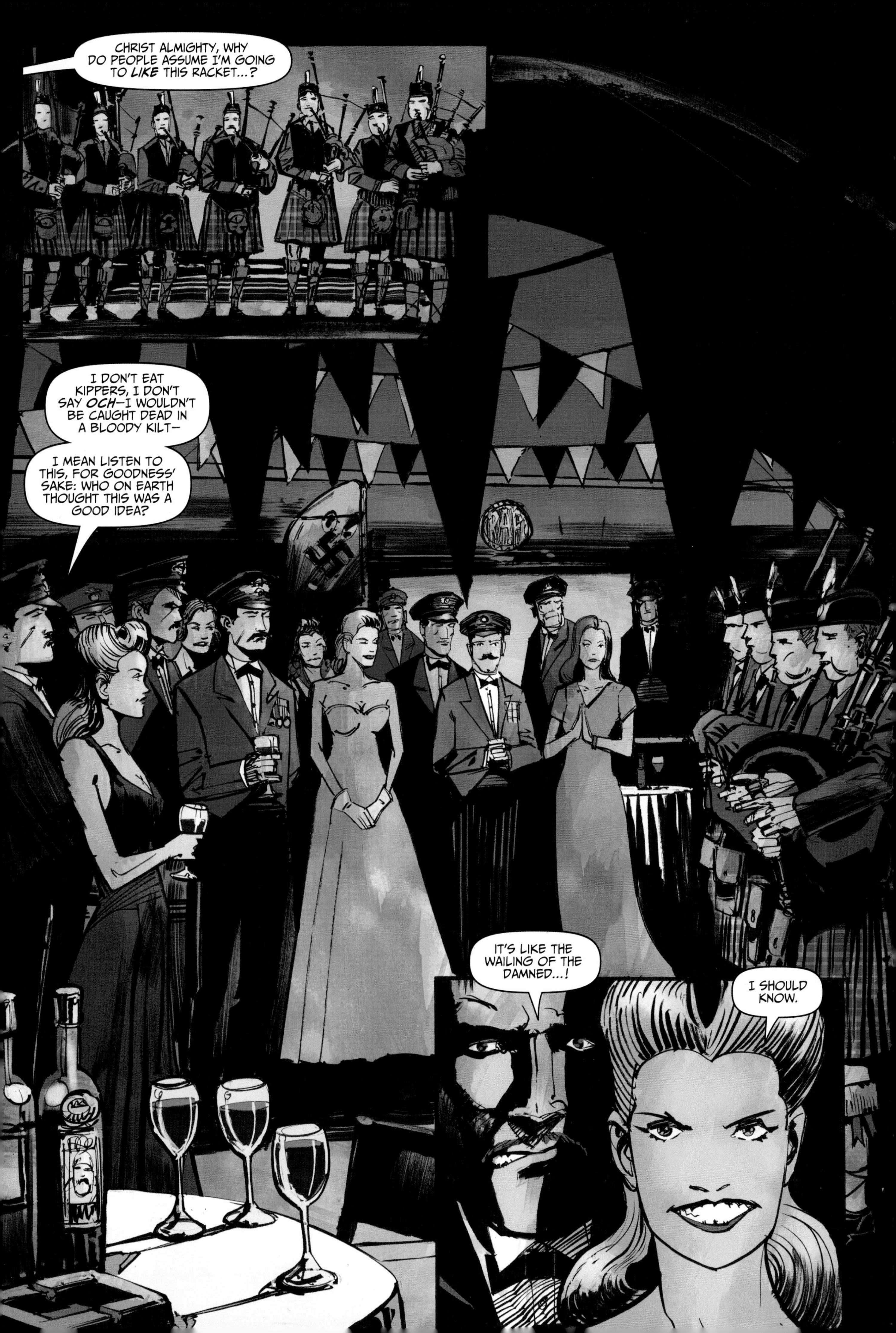

CHRIST ALMIGHTY, WHY DO PEOPLE ASSUME I'M GOING TO *LIKE* THIS RACKET...?
I DON'T EAT KIPPERS, I DON'T SAY *OCH*—I WOULDN'T BE CAUGHT DEAD IN A BLOODY KILT—
I MEAN LISTEN TO THIS, FOR GOODNESS' SAKE: WHO ON EARTH THOUGHT THIS WAS A GOOD IDEA?
RAF
IT'S LIKE THE WAILING OF THE DAMNED...!
I SHOULD KNOW.

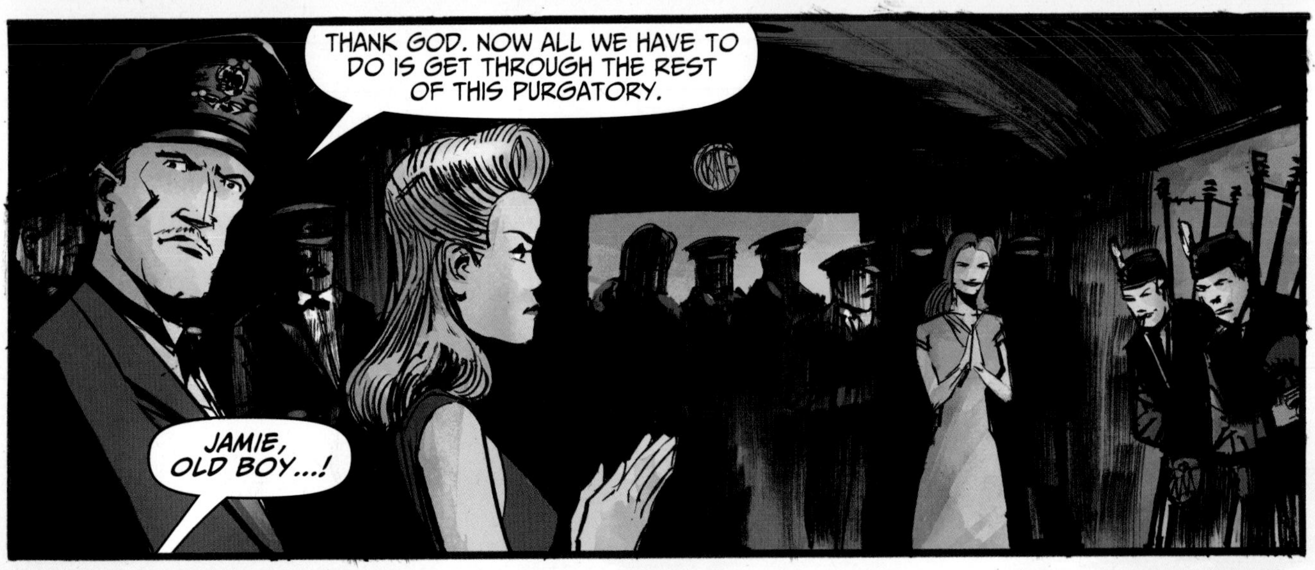
THANK GOD. NOW ALL WE HAVE TO DO IS GET THROUGH THE REST OF THIS PURGATORY.
JAMIE, OLD BOY...!

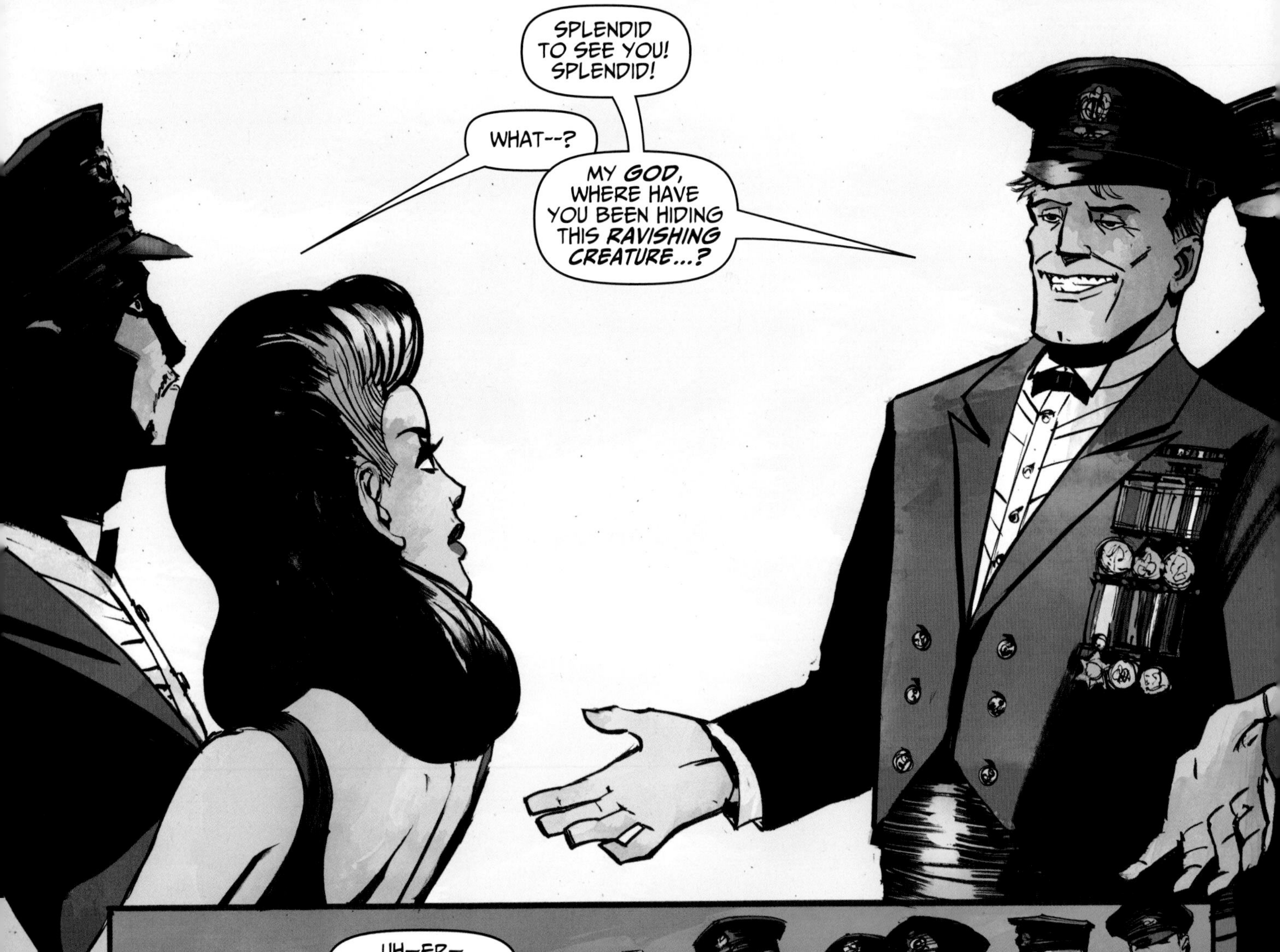
SPLENDID TO SEE YOU! SPLENDID!
WHAT--?
MY GOD, WHERE HAVE YOU BEEN HIDING THIS RAVISHING CREATURE...?

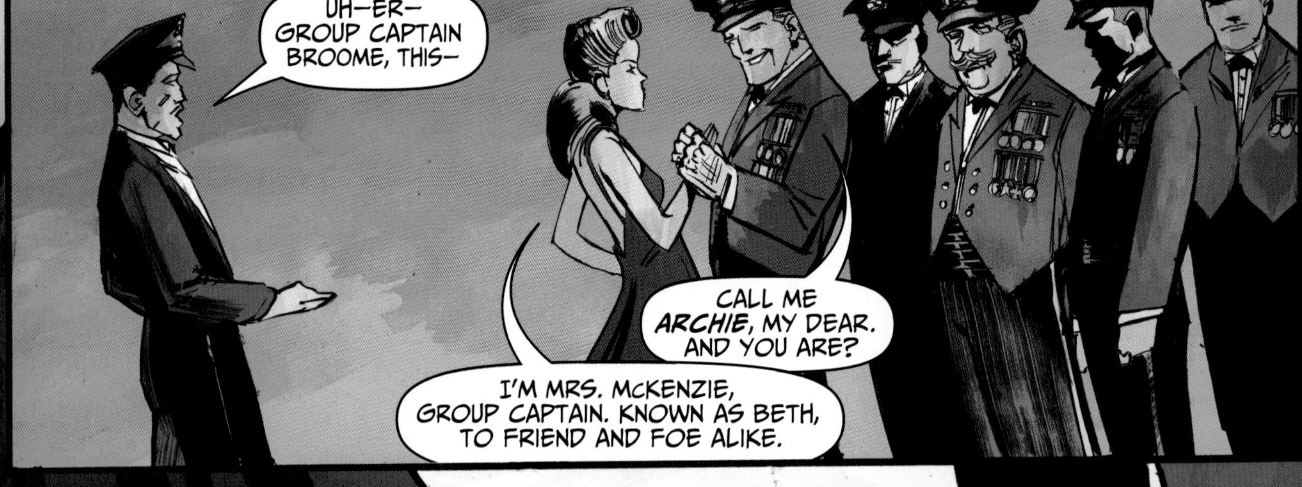
UH—ER— GROUP CAPTAIN BROOME, THIS—
CALL ME ARCHIE, MY DEAR. AND YOU ARE?
I'M MRS. McKENZIE, GROUP CAPTAIN. KNOWN AS BETH, TO FRIEND AND FOE ALIKE.

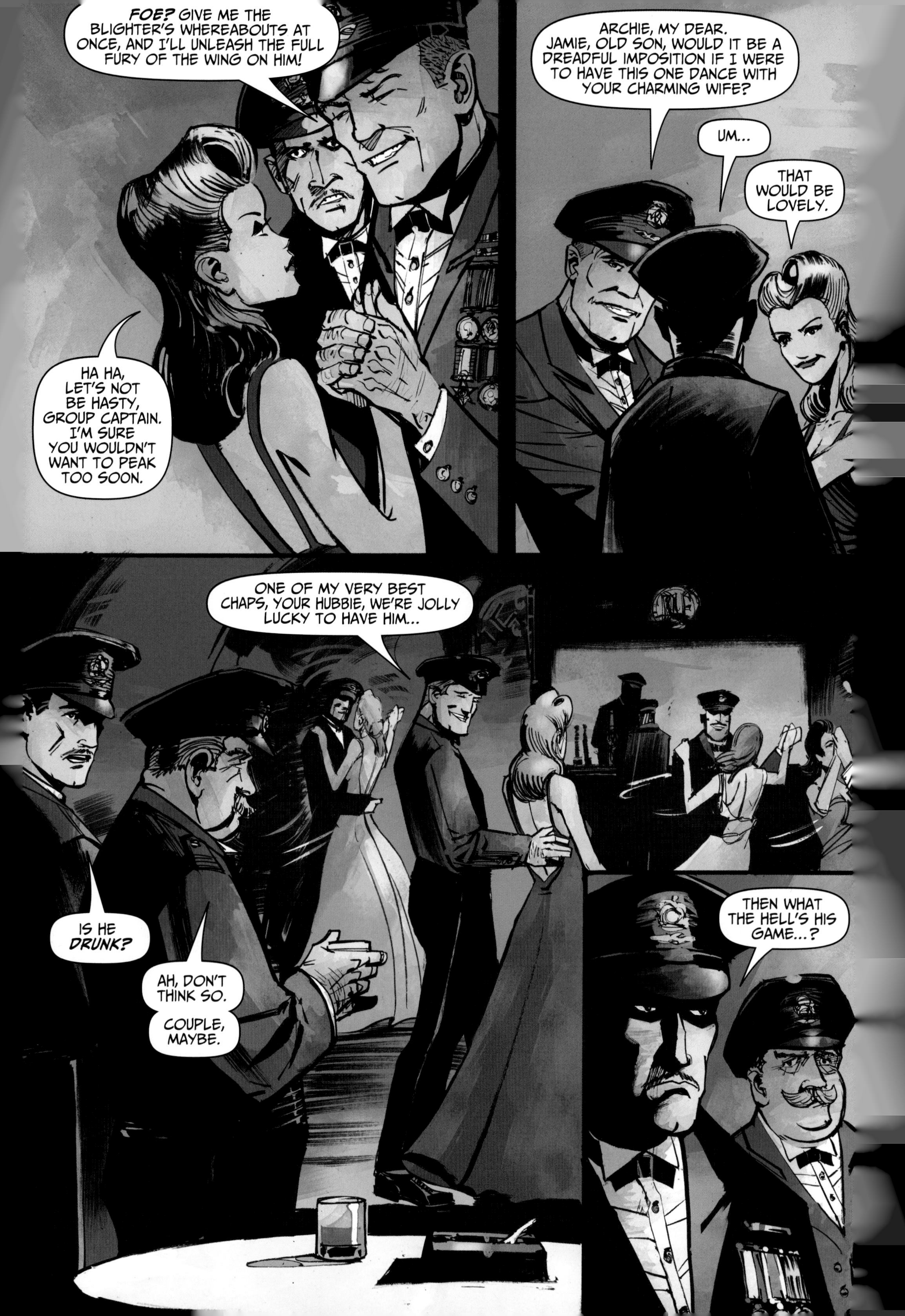
FOE? GIVE ME THE BLIGHTER'S WHEREABOUTS AT ONCE, AND I'LL UNLEASH THE FULL FURY OF THE WING ON HIM!
HA HA, LET'S NOT BE HASTY, GROUP CAPTAIN. I'M SURE YOU WOULDN'T WANT TO PEAK TOO SOON.
ARCHIE, MY DEAR. JAMIE, OLD SON, WOULD IT BE A DREADFUL IMPOSITION IF I WERE TO HAVE THIS ONE DANCE WITH YOUR CHARMING WIFE?
UM...
THAT WOULD BE LOVELY.
ONE OF MY VERY BEST CHAPS, YOUR HUBBIE, WE'RE JOLLY LUCKY TO HAVE HIM...
IS HE DRUNK?
AH, DON'T THINK SO.
COUPLE, MAYBE.
THEN WHAT THE HELL'S HIS GAME...?

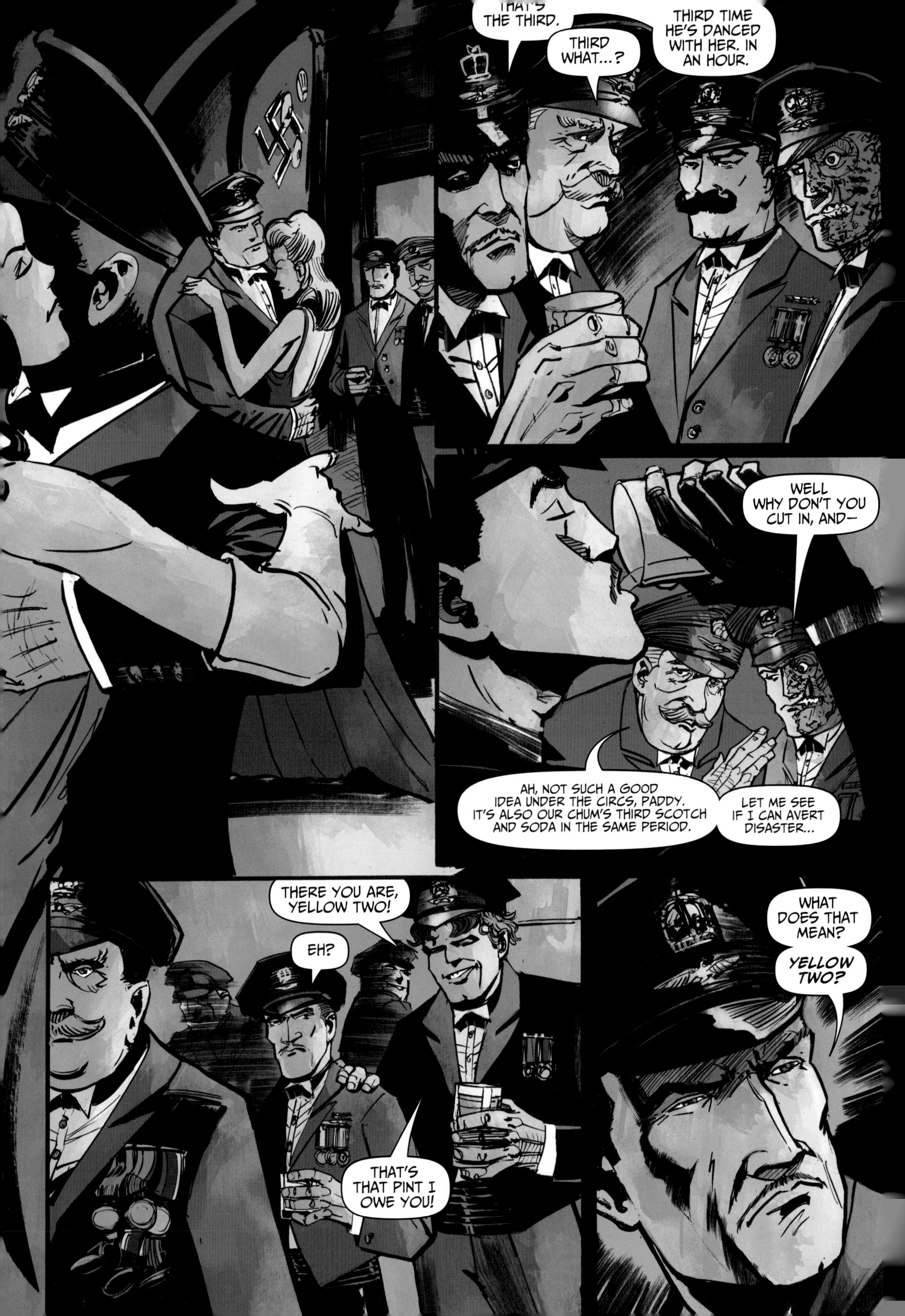
THAT'S THE THIRD.
THIRD WHAT...?
THIRD TIME HE'S DANCED WITH HER. IN AN HOUR.
WELL WHY DON'T YOU CUT IN, AND—
AH, NOT SUCH A GOOD IDEA UNDER THE CIRCS, PADDY. IT'S ALSO OUR CHUM'S THIRD SCOTCH AND SODA IN THE SAME PERIOD.
LET ME SEE IF I CAN AVERT DISASTER...
THERE YOU ARE, YELLOW TWO!
EH?
THAT'S THAT PINT I OWE YOU!
WHAT DOES THAT MEAN?
YELLOW TWO?

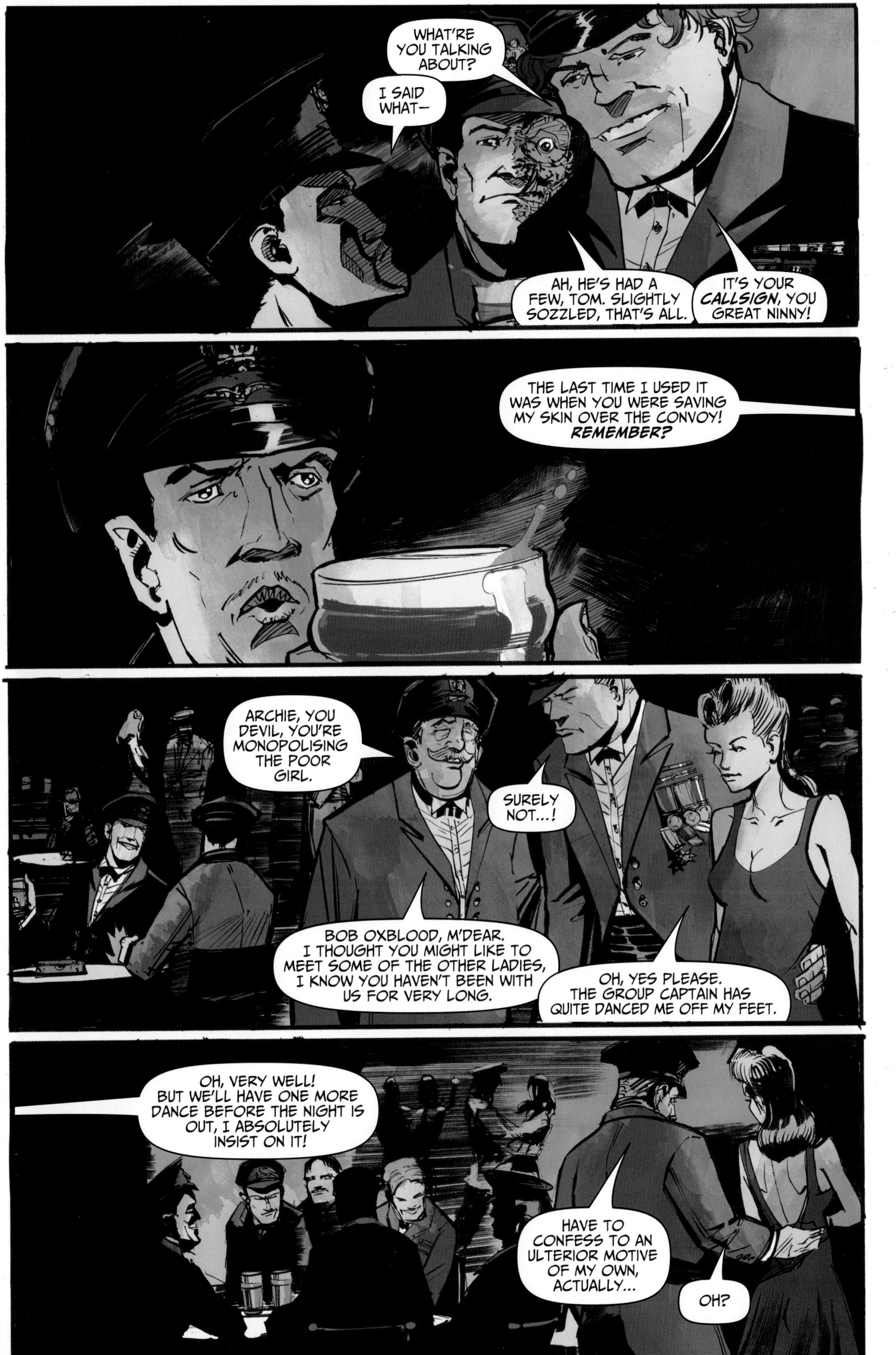
WHAT'RE YOU TALKING ABOUT?
I SAID WHAT–
AH, HE'S HAD A FEW, TOM. SLIGHTLY SOZZLED, THAT'S ALL.
IT'S YOUR CALLSIGN, YOU GREAT NINNY!
THE LAST TIME I USED IT WAS WHEN YOU WERE SAVING MY SKIN OVER THE CONVOY! REMEMBER?
ARCHIE, YOU DEVIL, YOU'RE MONOPOLISING THE POOR GIRL.
SURELY NOT...!
BOB OXBLOOD, M'DEAR. I THOUGHT YOU MIGHT LIKE TO MEET SOME OF THE OTHER LADIES, I KNOW YOU HAVEN'T BEEN WITH US FOR VERY LONG.
OH, YES PLEASE. THE GROUP CAPTAIN HAS QUITE DANCED ME OFF MY FEET.
OH, VERY WELL! BUT WE'LL HAVE ONE MORE DANCE BEFORE THE NIGHT IS OUT, I ABSOLUTELY INSIST ON IT!
HAVE TO CONFESS TO AN ULTERIOR MOTIVE OF MY OWN, ACTUALLY...
OH?

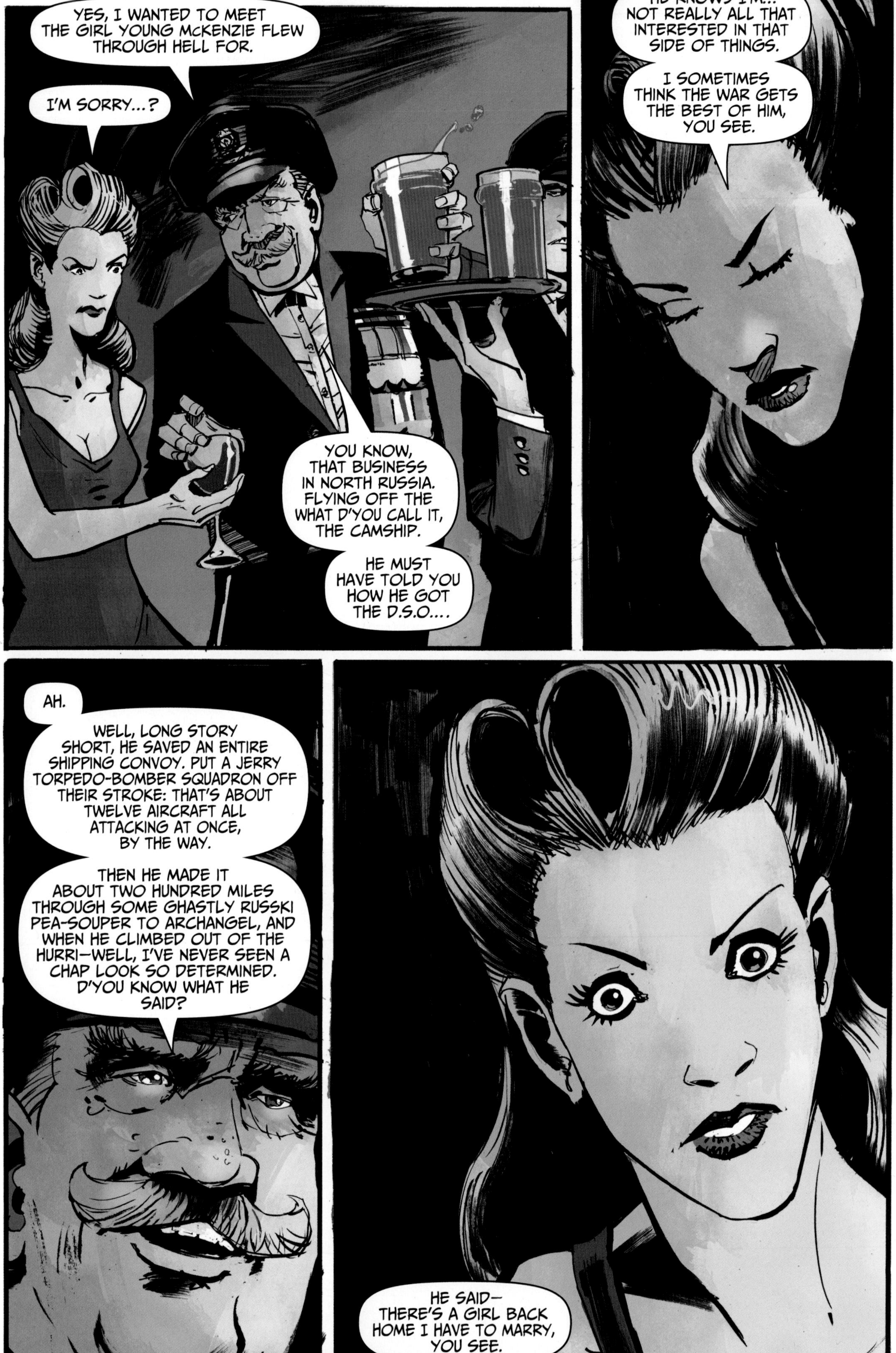
YES, I WANTED TO MEET THE GIRL YOUNG McKENZIE FLEW THROUGH HELL FOR.
I'M SORRY...?
YOU KNOW, THAT BUSINESS IN NORTH RUSSIA. FLYING OFF THE WHAT D'YOU CALL IT, THE CAMSHIP.
HE MUST HAVE TOLD YOU HOW HE GOT THE D.S.O....
HE KNOWS I'M... NOT REALLY ALL THAT INTERESTED IN THAT SIDE OF THINGS.
I SOMETIMES THINK THE WAR GETS THE BEST OF HIM, YOU SEE.
AH.
WELL, LONG STORY SHORT, HE SAVED AN ENTIRE SHIPPING CONVOY. PUT A JERRY TORPEDO-BOMBER SQUADRON OFF THEIR STROKE: THAT'S ABOUT TWELVE AIRCRAFT ALL ATTACKING AT ONCE, BY THE WAY.
THEN HE MADE IT ABOUT TWO HUNDRED MILES THROUGH SOME GHASTLY RUSSKI PEA-SOUPER TO ARCHANGEL, AND WHEN HE CLIMBED OUT OF THE HURRI—WELL, I'VE NEVER SEEN A CHAP LOOK SO DETERMINED. D'YOU KNOW WHAT HE SAID?
HE SAID— THERE'S A GIRL BACK HOME I HAVE TO MARRY, YOU SEE.

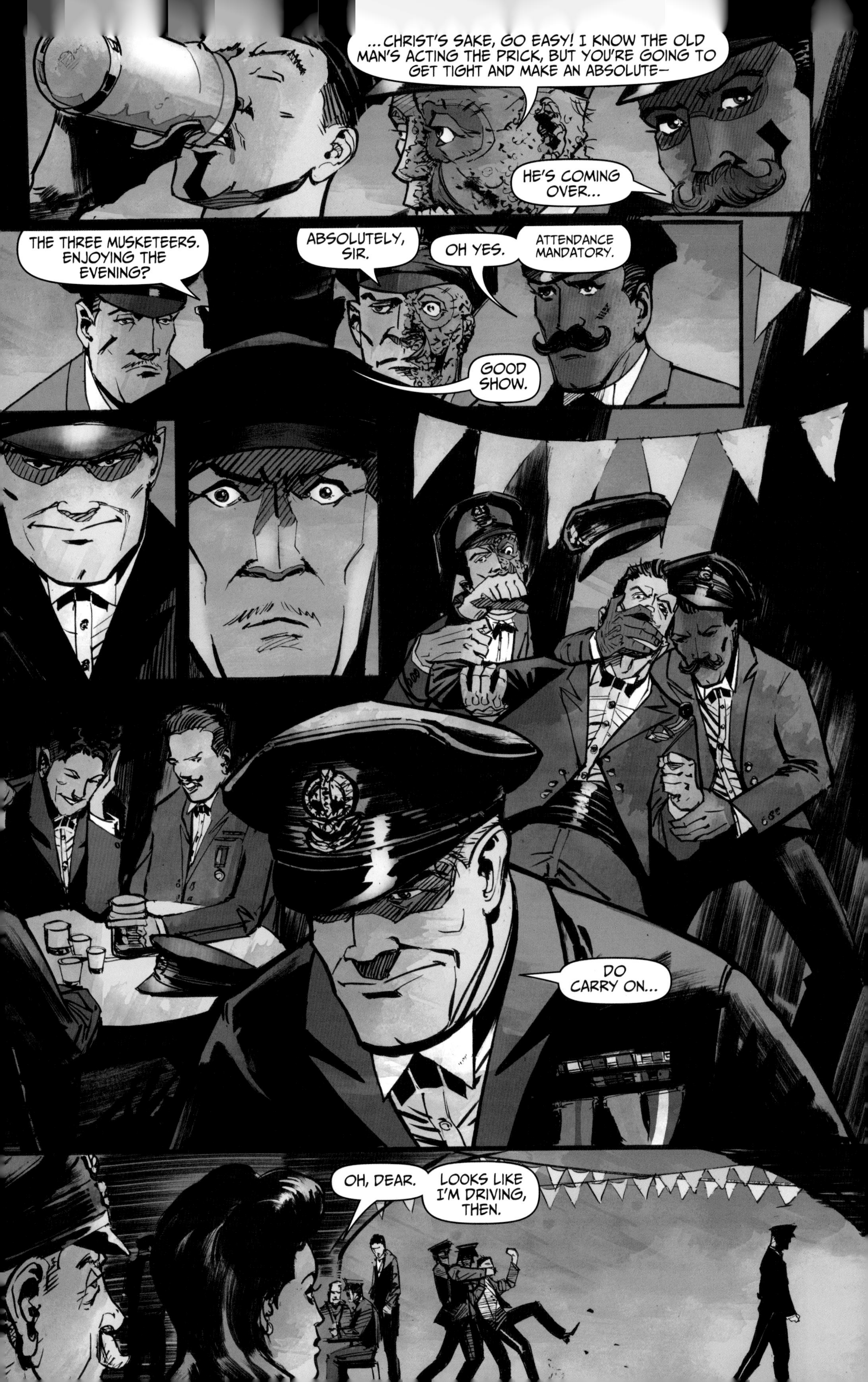
...CHRIST'S SAKE, GO EASY! I KNOW THE OLD MAN'S ACTING THE PRICK, BUT YOU'RE GOING TO GET TIGHT AND MAKE AN ABSOLUTE–
HE'S COMING OVER...
THE THREE MUSKETEERS. ENJOYING THE EVENING?
ABSOLUTELY, SIR.
OH YES.
ATTENDANCE MANDATORY.
GOOD SHOW.
DO CARRY ON...
OH, DEAR.
LOOKS LIKE I'M DRIVING, THEN.

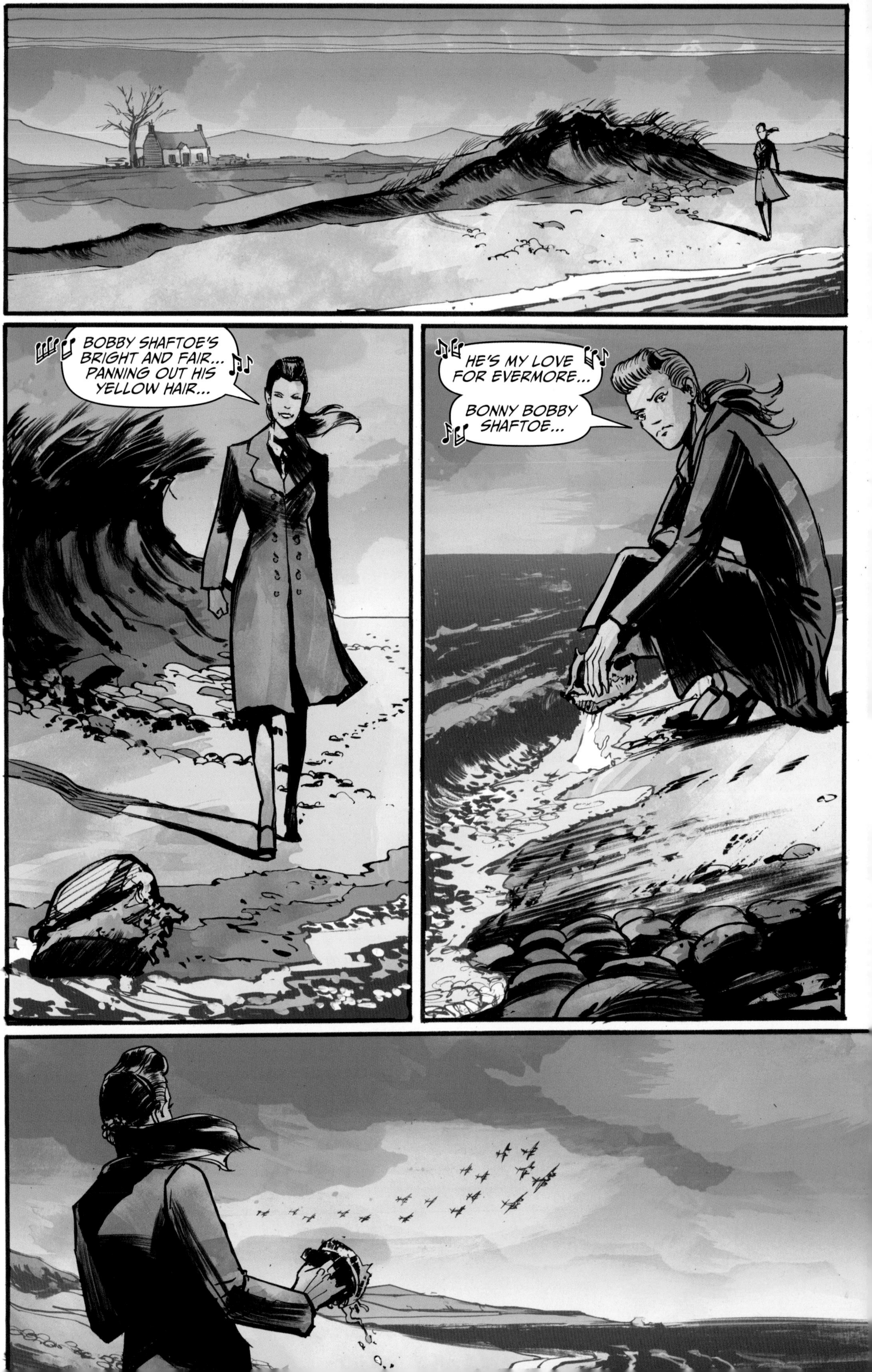
BOBBY SHAFTOE'S BRIGHT AND FAIR... PANNING OUT HIS YELLOW HAIR...
HE'S MY LOVE FOR EVERMORE...
BONNY BOBBY SHAFTOE...

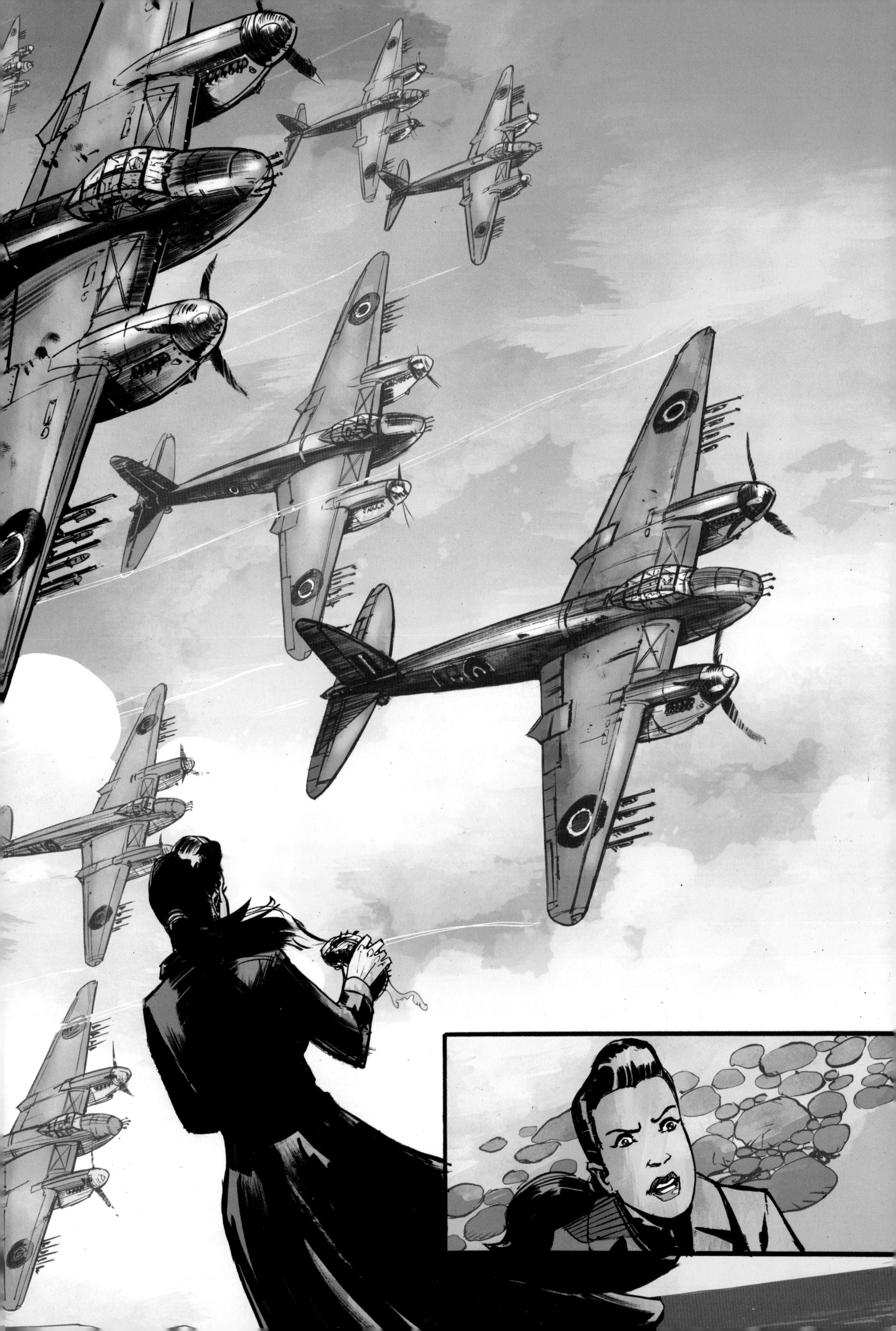

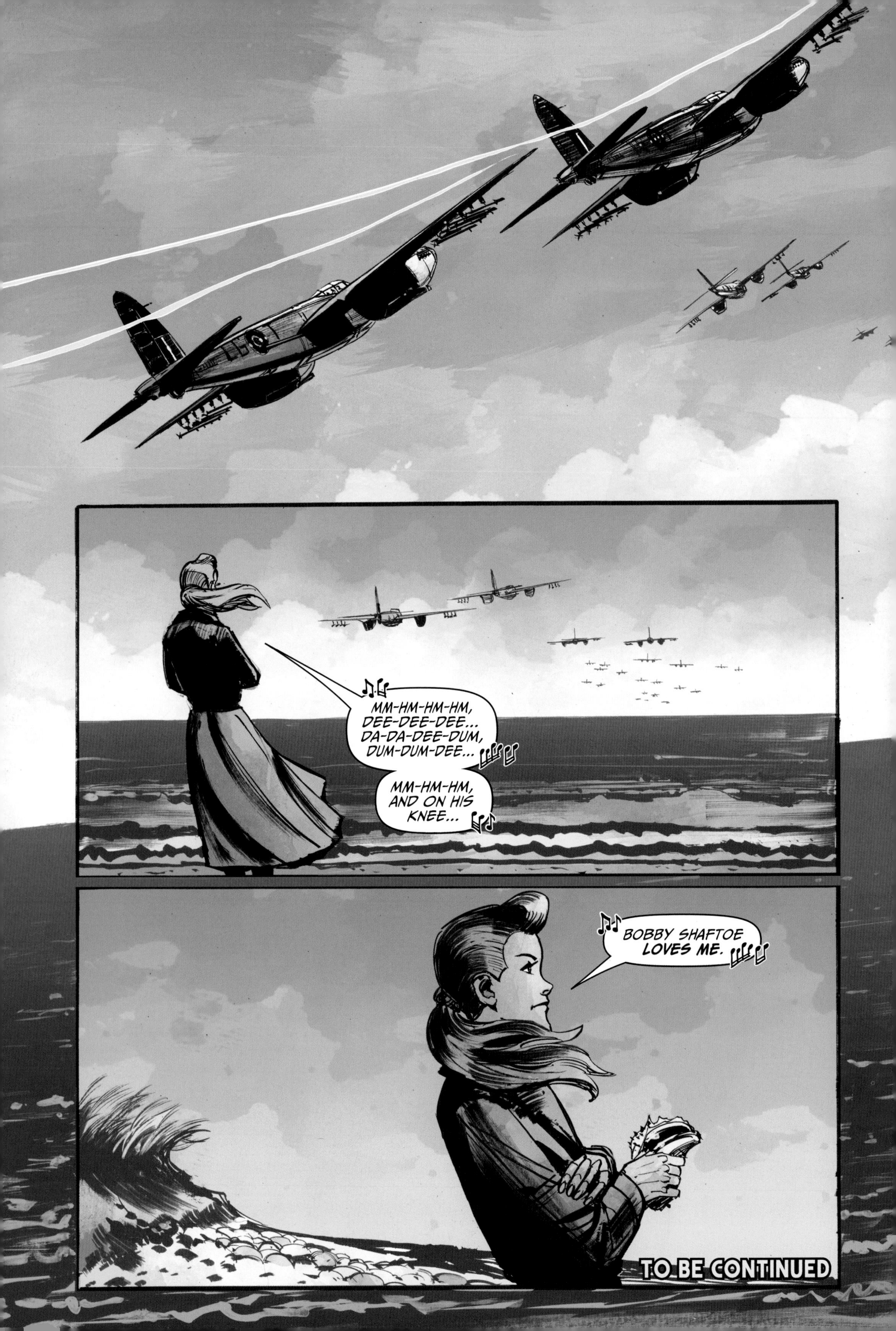
MM-HM-HM-HM, DEE-DEE-DEE... DA-DA-DEE-DUM, DUM-DUM-DEE...
MM-HM-HM, AND ON HIS KNEE...
BOBBY SHAFTOE LOVES ME.
TO BE CONTINUED

CHECK OUT THESE GREAT AFTERSHOCK
COLLECTIONS!

ALTERS VOL 1 & VOL 2
PAUL JENKINS / LEILA LEIZ   MAR171244 & APR181239

AMERICAN MONSTER VOL 1
BRIAN AZZARELLO / JUAN DOE   SEP161213

ANIMOSITY YEAR ONE, VOL 1, VOL 2 & VOL 3
MARGUERITE BENNETT / RAFAEL DE LATORRE   FEB181034, JAN171219, AUG171130 & MAY181314

ANIMOSITY: EVOLUTION VOL 1 & VOL 2
MARGUERITE BENNETT / ERIC GAPSTUR   MAR181079 & FEB188089

ANIMOSITY: THE RISE HARDCOVER
MARGUERITE BENNETT / JUAN DOE   AUG178324

ART OF JIM STARLIN HARDCOVER
JIM STARLIN   MAR181077

BABYTEETH VOL 1 & VOL 2
DONNY CATES / GARRY BROWN   OCT171087 & APR181225

BLACK-EYED KIDS VOL 1, VOL 2 & VOL 3
JOE PRUETT / SZYMON KUDRANSKI   AUG161115, FEB171100 & JAN181152

CAPTAIN KID VOL 1
MARK WAID / TOM PEYER / WILFREDO TORRES   APR171231

DARK ARK VOL 1
CULLEN BUNN / JUAN DOE   FEB181035

DREAMING EAGLES HARDCOVER
GARTH ENNIS / SIMON COLEBY   AUG161114

ELEANOR & THE EGRET VOL 1
JOHN LAYMAN / SAM KIETH   DEC171041

FU JITSU VOL 1
JAI NITZ / WESLEY ST. CLAIRE   APR181241

INSEXTS YEAR ONE, VOL 1 & VOL 2
MARGUERITE BENNETT / ARIELA KRISTANTINA   APR181228, JUN161072 & SEP171098

JIMMY'S BASTARDS VOL 1
GARTH ENNIS / RUSS BRAUN   DEC171040

PESTILENCE VOL 1
FRANK TIERI / OLEG OKUNEV   NOV171154

REPLICA VOL 1
PAUL JENKINS / ANDY CLARKE   MAY161030

ROUGH RIDERS VOL 1 & VOL 2
ADAM GLASS / PATRICK OLLIFFE   OCT161101 & SEP171097

SECOND SIGHT VOL 1
DAVID HINE / ALBERTO PONTICELLI   DEC161186

SHOCK VOL 1 HARDCOVER
VARIOUS   MAY161029

SUPERZERO VOL 1
AMANDA CONNER / JIMMY PALMIOTTI / RAFAEL DE LATORRE   MAY161029

UNHOLY GRAIL VOL 1
CULLEN BUNN / MIRKO COLAK   JAN181151

WORLD READER VOL 1
JEFF LOVENESS / JUAN DOE   SEP171096

**FIND THESE AT YOUR FAVORITE LOCAL COMIC
BOOK SHOP OR BOOK STORE! MORE INFO:**
www.aftershockcomics.com/collections

Each series Copyright © 2018 by their respective owners. All rights reserved.
AfterShock Comics and its logos are trademarks of AfterShock Comics, LLC.

ABOUT THE CREATORS OF

Out of the BLUE ™

GARTH ENNIS
writer

Garth Ennis has been writing comics since 1989. His credits include *Preacher*, *The Boys*, *Crossed*, *Battlefields and War Stories*, and successful runs on *The Punisher* and *Fury* for Marvel Comics. Originally from Belfast, Northern Ireland, he now lives in New York City with his wife, Ruth.

Keith Burns
artist

Keith Burns is an award-winning aviation artist and commercial illustrator. He has illustrated comics for the past decade with *Johnny Red* being the most recent. In 2012 he joined the Guild of Aviation Artists. In 2015 he won the Messier Dowty award for best acrylic painting in show. In 2016 he was made a full member of the Guild, had his first solo exhibition at the RAF Club in London and won Aviation Painting of the Year. In 1996 Keith was encouraged to leave his chosen degree course in fine arts because he couldn't paint or draw. He is currently illustrating the *Ladybird* WW2 series written by James Holland.

JASON WORDIE
colorist

Colorist Jason Wordie hails from Canada. He has done work for Image, Dark Horse, Boom!, Titan and Vault. Some of his works include *God Country*, *Abbott*, *Wasted Space*, *Penny Dreadful*, *Turncoat* and *Grafity's Wall*.

ROB STEEN
letterer

Rob Steen is the illustrator of the *Flanimals* series of children's books written by Ricky Gervais and the Garth Ennis children's book *Erf*. He is also the colorist of David Hine's graphic novel *Strange Embrace* and letterer of comic books for AfterShock, Marvel, Dynamite, Image, and First Second.